HUMANITY
in
PERIL

Current Conditions in Education

Through the Eyes of a HS Principal

D1606111

Rick Lasley

outskirts
press

To ALL current educators
still working today:

Hang in there—
keep your head up
and hang on to hope that help is on the way …

Preface

Back in the day, it was common for kids to "find their own fun" while playing outside, and the fun became something as simple as kicking a tin can around. I can remember doing this on occasion growing up myself; if not a *tin* can, I can definitely remember dishing out some punishment on aluminum cans.

If you ever have had the privilege of taking on this "entertainment" and spent any time at it like I did, you would find out after some time that the can quickly deteriorates and it reaches a point that it is no longer intact enough to keep your attention. At this point, most kids move on to find some other form of entertainment. I can remember as a kid wondering how many more kicks it would take for the can to disappear into shrapnel.

EDUCATION, today, represents this "can" that has been kicked to the point that it is soon to become unrecognizable, if it hasn't already reached that point. **THIS** is the reason that I made the decision to publish my journal ...

On the first day of school in August 2021, I was sitting on the back deck talking to my wife, Angela. I was using her as a sounding board, letting her know of all the troubles that we had getting all the teachers hired to start the year and how we were starting the year with four open custodial positions as well as five open cafeteria positions. The first full pandemic year (2020– 2021) had been extremely difficult and had taken its toll on a number of good teachers, who had made the decision to retire a little earlier than they had originally planned. Although we all hoped and anticipated that THIS year would be better (at LEAST we were starting the year with students IN school!), my concern was that the trend of teachers leaving the profession would only get worse.

I made the decision while venting to my wife that this would be my last year in education (making a total of 32 years). I also decided that I would write this journal and make entries as often as I felt the need to reflect on experiences that unfolded for that day, or, just VENT …

So, the journal took a life of its own and soon became more than just "therapy" to get me through the year. After trends became apparent regarding student behavior and "rock star" teachers feeling more overwhelmed than I had ever witnessed, it seemed that this journal might actually have a higher purpose than to simply provide me therapy. After tragic events had taken place at Apollo HS, after continued concerns with student absenteeism and the trouble we were having with our youngest students engaging in learning, I reached out to some of my most trusted educator confidants for advice and I sent them the first-quarter journal entries …

Now that this journal exists, whom may you ask will it most benefit? While educators alike should all empathize and relate to the stories within, I feel the most benefit for reading this journal would be community members and especially our legislators. This journal should be considered the "sounding of an alarm" and a quick call to action ... OR, there may not be anyone left (***certified*** as a teacher) to teach our children in five to ten years. If my analogy of education representing the tin can being kicked down the road until it is unrecognizable is in any way accurate, this could very well happen!

Whoever chooses to read this journal, please consider the following facts (at least as far as I can relate to Kentucky and especially the region with which I can most associate) as you read the events that unfold to make up the Fall Semester 2021 at Apollo HS:

- The pipeline supplying K– 12 teaching candidates had reached a trickle in most areas of the state ***before*** the pandemic ever started. At the HS level especially, in some areas there were NO applicants to apply for open positions. ***After*** the start of the pandemic, there are districts that have reached the same problem only at the K– 3 level. Consider the thought that NO candidates apply to teach at an elementary school when there is a 2nd- grade teacher opening.

- Anxiety, depression, and the overall emotional/mental status of our students had become a growing concern ***before*** the pandemic ever started. The pandemic has changed ALL of us, but the group that it has affected the most is our students. This explains a lot of the "extreme" behavior that is depicted in several entries of this journal.

- In Kentucky, education and teachers in particular have taken a beating and been "dragged through the mud" via social- media platforms and even certain politicians. The words and actions of Kentucky's former governor with the threat of removing sick days and dismantling the retirement system greatly reduced the number of teacher candidates graduating from colleges and universities ***in the years leading up to the pandemic***.

- The cost-of-living increases for educators have not kept up with the rest of society in the past ten years. The SEEK formula has not been funded enough by the government so that districts can safely increase pay to the level that educators deserve. I have known teachers who have had a second job (albeit part-time) just to make ends meet and pay off their college loans. How long will this trend continue when these pandemic conditions exist for teachers?

- In most Kentucky districts, cafeteria workers and custodians make somewhere between $12– $13.50 per hour. We all know how hard it has become for fast-food restaurants to maintain their "workforce" when the offer is as much as $14 per hour! As of Jan. 1, 2022, the minimum wage in Illinois (as well as other states) became $12 per hour.

With ALL this in mind, I certainly hope that you can read the contents of this journal and "hear" the sounding of the alarm. More than this, I hope that you are one who is prepared to step up and help take action for what is needed **_to give education the RESPECT and APPEAL that it deserves_**. Please keep in mind that this will not happen overnight. Case in point: if the number of students entering the college/ university teacher prep programs **_doubled_** to start the next semester, the outcome of teacher candidates to fill the "pipeline" would happen a minimum of three or four years later ...

I would like to take the time to thank my family; my wife Angela, and my four children Todd, Troy, Lauren, and Aaron, for their support over my 32-year career in education. Being the dedicated person I was to my job as an educator, coach, and administrator, I was not one to have my summers off. There were times I regretfully missed family functions because of my work, but my family was always there to show their love and support for the passion I committed to educating and starting young adults on their life's path. I love you all and I appreciate your love and understanding.

I would be remiss not to include thanks to my parents, Anthony and Sheila Lasley, for they are the ones who were most instrumental in developing my work ethic and my compassion for others. Growing up on a dairy farm in White Mills, Kentucky, we worked harder before lunch than most people do in a week and there was no such thing as "time off". We were surrounded by a community of farmers who made time to connect and help each other when it was necessary. It was a hard life, but it was a very good life that I appreciate far more today than I did when I was growing up. Little did I know the sweat and the toil that I left behind on that farm is exactly what developed me into the person I am today. Thank you, Mom and Dad, for everything you did for me growing up and always allowing me to make my own decisions for my life's journey and the path I have taken. I love you both.

I would like to thank Dr. Rhonda Caldwell, Executive Director of the Kentucky Association of School Administrators (KASA), for her advice and support for writing and publishing this book. Rhonda has been a constant guide and supporter of all administrators since her connection to KASA, but I appreciate her time and attention she has afforded me over my twenty years as an administrator. It is through her counsel, her commitment to leadership and growth, that has been instrumental in keeping me in the arena for the time that I have. Thank you, Rhonda, for believing in the leadership that Kentucky administration provides and for your support and friendship.

I would also like to thank Mr. Eddie Price, retired teacher, whom I had the pleasure of working with in the Hancock Co. school system for eight years, and author of books like *Widder's Landing*. I have a lot of respect for Eddie Price, for the tremendous teacher that he was in the classroom. He was a "rock star" who easily connected with students and made history so ***fascinating*** that he made his students (even the unmotivated) *want* to be a part of his class! Eddie helped with the first edit of this book and also walked me through the publishing process as a first-time author. Thank you, Eddie, for your dedication to teaching and your guidance in getting this first publication of mine off the ground ...

I hope you enjoy reading the contents of this journal and agree to help restore the **Gateway of Humanity** that Education is and was always intended to be! ...

Author's Note

Other than my wife and children, the names of any individuals mentioned in this book have been changed to protect their identity. Most names have been withheld for the same reason.

August 11, 2021 (My LAST First Day) – There comes a time when you just know. After 32 *first* days of high school as an educator, so many things have changed. Today was special in that we had 1,400+ students walking into the building for the first day of school, ALL masked and nervous about so many things **other than** that first-day- of- school feeling. Unlike the experience that we had one year ago as the bells of 1st period rang and the eerie silence of no students in the building. The Covid -19 pandemic was nearing a peak with so many unknowns in front of us. Last year was the most difficult experience I have ever seen in education, but I could not bring myself to end my career on that note. Unlike many other educators who chose to finish earlier than originally planned, I decided I had to finish on a more positive note …

On this special day, I squashed a bug for one of our senior students, "Tommy," who falls well within the autism spectrum and has also experienced his share of trauma that he carries with him as he enters the halls of Apollo HS every day. He worries constantly about a LOT of things and has a profound fear of anything that crawls. Although he is one that all adults at Apollo know is someone who will consume a lot of your time, I was happy to see him and to take care of the poor beetle who found himself at the wrong place at the wrong time. My apologies to the beetle …

I also ran into "Darren," who was clearly happy to see me AND not only grasped my hand in welcome, but also pulled me in for a firm "bro-hug" that lasted long enough for me to realize today wasn't the day for his bath. "Darren" was the young man that I distinctly remember walking into the office on Friday, March 13, 2020, as students were departing the building for what would be the last time that students were present for that school year. **None** of us thought at the time that this "pause " for virtual learning would last more than a couple of weeks. We would all come back after Spring Break and all would resume as normal and we would finish the year. It never happened. "Darren" gave me a hug on that day as well. It caught me by surprise, and I have since wondered what prompted that hug. "Darren" didn't make a habit of hugging me or any others that I can recall. Was it his need for reassurance that "everything would be OK"? Or, was it his reassurance to me that we were going to be fine and that we would see each other later? "Darren" is another one of our special-needs students who has many challenges and also presents as many challenges to the adults who work with him, putting more effort into finding ways to avoid work than the time he puts into his modified work load. Never send "Darren" on a mission ... it would always take him most of the day to get there.

On this last first day of school, we had an opportunity for a "restart" as we try to recover learning from this past year. It was overall a "good" first day of school ... Only a "glitch" or two, defined to be ... some **veteran** teachers not following explicit, simple instructions for handing out schedules 1st period to the students and NOT counting ANY students absent in Infinite Campus (rules we have followed for eons?) ... teachers NOT following the special bell and lunch schedule for the day (upperclassmen coming to lunch when it should have only been freshmen) ... students wearing unimaginable clothing, like the young lady wearing a corset for her top and carrying a book bag that had depictions of the many stages of women's breasts all over it ... and (a FIRST for me), an employee thinking that professional "jeans or better" (along with the DCPS t-shirt we were all asked to wear) allowed her to wear her "Daisy Dukes"!?! Yes, so many things have changed!

We got them to school. We fed them. We got them all home, unharmed. It **_was_** a good first day ...

August 13, 2021 – Not enough money in education … The day started with the mother of a 9th-grade student who decided to pay a visit because the family was going to refuse wearing a mask and force us to make a decision on her daughter's education. Sadly, this mother's understanding of an **Executive Order** given by the Governor of Kentucky was "just a suggestion". Little did we at Apollo HS know that the father was making the same stand at the middle school and elementary schools where their younger children were attending school. Keeping the conversation as short as possible, the decision that our district had made regarding this situation was for students to either wear a mask OR parents homeschool. We made this offer and then had to have our School Resource Officer escort mom and her daughter out of the building. Incidentally, mom was wearing a "F**k the World" t-shirt. FAR too many of our parents today base ALL of their information on what they hear from social media …

———— ♦ ————

Down four custodians and not enough cafeteria ladies to serve our 1,500 students. This has been the "theme" so far as we have started this 2022 school year continuing to work through the pandemic. Apollo HS was fortunate to be able to hire all **certified** positions that were posted at the end of the school year and during the summer. Because this nation has kicked the can down the road as long as it has (lack of funding to support both certified and classified raises to keep up with the cost of living), there are very few applicants for schools to interview. In some cases, there are NO certified applicants available and districts are stuck finding candidates with a BA degree but no teacher training/certification ("Option 6" candidates). Sometimes, we are lucky to find even those individuals.

This can-kicking has been an issue long before the beginning of the coronavirus. The pandemic has only magnified the issue because of the inflation that has been created by the government "support for all" initiatives. With inflation and the cost of common everyday items, food, and the cost of lumber soaring as high as it has these past six months, who can afford to work a job like custodian, bus driver, or cafeteria worker in a school system for $12 to $13.50 per hour? Again, the government needs to help and stop kicking the can. School districts only have so much money to fund salaries. Most of the public is unaware that a typical district uses around 85% of its budget on salaries **_alone_**. The districts cannot just decide to offer their employees raises.

Apollo HS has eleven custodians on staff to effectively clean, disinfect, and maintain the building (3 custodians during the day and 8 custodians for the evening— ALL responsible for maintaining 150,000 square feet). Even before the pandemic started, Apollo HS has had a hard time filling all of the custodial positions. In my five years as principal at Apollo HS, I have hired 25 custodians. These positions have been a revolving door as candidates either find something better after working two or three months or they find out that it is too much work and area to cover for what they are being paid. The district has made attempts to use a cleaning service only to find that the cleaning service is not at all equipped to clean school systems.

So, as we enter the first week of the new school year, I find myself securing the help of our teachers to help straighten their rooms (all trash off the floor, chairs on tables, and trash bagged up and ready at the door) at the end of each day. The Command Chief of Apollo's Air Force Junior ROTC program offered the assistance of the cadets to go to all areas of the building to collect the trash and have all trash in the toters ready for the custodians to wheel out to the dumpster.

We have also found alternative means of cleaning up after home ball games so that the custodial staff can focus on the cleaning of our restrooms and classrooms. This is one aspect of high school custodial pay that must change— the many evening events that require extra attention and cleaning multiple times per week. The fact that all of a district's elementary custodial positions are filled before the high school custodial positions is no coincidence. Both elementary and high school custodians get the same pay! In the elementary world, the school building typically becomes a "ghost town" by 5:00 pm and the evening custodian(s) are left to do their work uninterrupted. During fall sports season (with volleyball games) and especially winter sports seasons (girls and boys basketball, wrestling, cheerleading, and some-times indoor track), it is rare that there are not at least two home events where the custodians have to drop what they are doing in their classrooms to all meet in the gym to collectively clean the area at around 9:30. Their evening shift ends at 11:30 or midnight.

In this past year in trying to hire custodians, we have had three candi-dates agree to be interviewed only to not show up for the interview. Any effort to try to contact the individuals (if nothing else checking to see that they had the correct day/time) proved to be pointless. On one particular occasion, we had interviewed a gentleman and offered him the position. We were excited because this candidate had custodial experience and he lived in the area! The next day he called to decline the position, stating that he had been made the offer to work at an elementary school in a neighboring district. Enough said? There is NOT enough money in education ...

———•◆•———

Near the end of this Friday the 13th, a parent of one of our seniors who is signed up for Ag Co-op called and demanded she speak with the principal. Upon taking her call in my office, this parent immediately proceeded to "lawyer-up" and demanded to know the name of the teacher who allowed her juvenile daughter to leave campus without her permission (her daughter turns 18 in 60 days). In my conversation with her, she made several demands and mentioned that she was going to speak with the superintendent, along with her lawyer. Each time that I made an attempt to speak, she cut me off and made more demands.

Because I hadn't even had an opportunity to speak with the teacher in question (while she continued to rant about something), I hung up. I needed to find out from the teacher responsible for this student what was going on. As soon as I did, I made an attempt to call the mother back, but this spiraled out of control to the point that mother and daughter showed up at school with the proper paperwork needed for Ag Co-op signed. Because she was hostile, our secretary at the front desk would not let her in (we have a security system in place that allows our secretary to "buzz" people into the office, once they and their purpose for visiting is identified).

I came to the front door and opened it without allowing the parent to come inside the office. I asked this mother if we could have a civil conversation— otherwise, there was no point in continuing the conversation. She immediately picked up where she'd left off in our phone conversation and went further, calling me by my first name, mocking the fact that I did not share with her the Ag teacher's first name. I told her that we were not on a first- name basis and asked our School Resource Officer to escort her out of the building.

This entire situation and conversation should have been SIMPLE. There *is* paperwork and parent signatures are required before a student can start Ag Co-op and leave early to go to work instead of attending classes. The Ag teacher had allowed the daughter to go obtain her father's signature and the irrational, completely belligerent mother did not know why she was out of school without her permission.

There is NOT enough money in education! ...

August 16, 2021 (First Monday of the school year) – Unlike the previous Friday that began and ended with irrational parents, this day felt "normal". Although, picking up from the previous day's theme of being understaffed in schools, I had to spend my fourth day as a cashier at lunch time to help alleviate the cafeteria shortage.

We have nearly 1,500 students at Apollo HS and all of them need the opportunity to eat. While a small portion of our students take advantage of the hot breakfast items that our ladies cook and serve every morning, at least 90% of our population take part in the lunch program, which offers a variety of cuisines and five serving lines. It takes a minimum number of cooks and line servers to pull this off, as well as five cashiers available to scan and charge each student appropriately. Whatever that minimum number of staff has been, Apollo HS has fallen short all four days of school so far ...

Although we definitely need more staff to help our ladies do their phenomenal job of feeding our students, I can't say that I am complaining about helping them out. In all honesty, on most days I have done this, it is the BEST part of my day! I have the ability to directly interact with as much as 20% of our population of students, many of which can't break the habit of going to the same line EVERY day. It doesn't take long to see this group of students come through enough that you get to know them by name, giving me the opening to build a rapport with students I would have otherwise never known. It reminds me of teaching and the opportunities I had in the classroom to get to know MY students. It is for reasons like this, I have **_missed the classroom_** for almost 20 years of my career!

As much as I enjoy being a cashier, HERE is the problem— I cannot do my job as principal of a large HS when I am tied down to a cash register for 90 minutes of our school day. I cannot just leave the register halfway through the line of students if someone needs my attention. I cannot visit classrooms and help guide our newly hired teachers during the period that our lunch is served. ALL things as principal get put on hold (minus emergencies, of course) when I am helping the cafeteria ladies.

Don't get me wrong, if the cafeteria manager comes to me pleading for help the next 182 school days, I will do the exact same thing that I have done the first four school days. It's the lack of understanding of anyone outside of the school when it comes to why certain things have not been accomplished to their liking, that we have missed deadlines for teacher evaluations, etc., that I have the biggest problem with. So many things have changed about serving as principal of a high school, and there are so many people outside of the school building who have completely lost touch with what the job now entails or, especially, how to effectively help principals do the work that we were hired to do.

As an administrator entering my 20th year, you would think that **_expe-rience_** would eventually help make the job easier to *manage*. Quite the contrary. Yes, the pandemic has certainly magnified the issues that I have spoken of, but there are so many things that are different about the job (**_not at all related_** to the pandemic) that have completely changed the role of principal. **_Every year_** I have been principal has brought a little more challenge than the one before. The BIGGEST issue creating the most challenge in education today is the shortage of custodian candidates, shortage of cafeteria candidates, AND, especially, the shortage of certified teachers to put into our classrooms. How much longer can education endure this trend?

August 18, 2021 – We have completed our first five days of the school year and most everyone has established routines. "Darren" sought me out this morning and found me in an office close to our Commons Area. Taking off his mask and getting close to me, he asks, "Notice anything different?" Not noticing anything much different, I decided to throw him a bone: "YOU'VE SHAVED!! Looking good, Darren!" He turned around as if his sole mission for the day had been accomplished and headed for his crew to hang out before classes started. It is the simplest interactions with students that do an educator's soul good— I may or may not have made Darren's day, but I can tell you that simple exchange made me smile inside and out.

Another booster-shot for the educator's soul is to be surrounded by dynamic and dedicated educators. I have been fortunate in my career to either find myself in that position or I have had the opportunity to **_place_** dynamic people in positions that they are suited for. The best part of my job is to start conversations that lead to good results by way of involving the dynamic people and throwing them the reins to take control. The **_hardest_** part of the job is finding a way to never say "no" when these individuals ask for funding to make some aspect of their plan or idea come true. After twenty years as an administrator, you learn to become creative ...

This morning, as I revealed that "Darren" had practiced some good hygiene, I had stopped by to see our two instructional coaches. These two are "Dynamos" (note the capital 'D')! Whether I "placed" these two in their positions or they were headed there anyway, it doesn't matter. The impact that these two individuals have on instructional support for new teachers, teachers of English Language Learners (ELLs), and best-practice teaching strategies in general is a blessing to Apollo. Too many things have happened since I spoke with them this morning for me to remember the content of our conversation as I type this journal entry. This is a good illustration of my point— whatever we discussed put me further in a good mood because they had resolved to take on the task and make it part of their mission. "Dynamos"! ...

Another aspect of my job that I thoroughly enjoy is hearing ideas from students that we adults are too busy and preoccupied to come up with. I heard an awesome idea from one of our seniors this morning ...

Apollo is in the midst of major construction of a new addition to the building, as well as future renovations to the existing and original building (est. 1969). In all, there will be construction going on **_within_** Apollo HS for the next three school years. At the start of this school year, we were supposed to have moved into the new addition and start "shuffling" teachers out of certain original areas one semester at a time to allow for renovation to take place. Poor planning and inadequate workforce support to complete the original timeline forced the new building project into "overtime". What DID happen, after lighting some "fires" and applying a little force, is the connector between the original building— the most recent upgrade to the campus— and the new building reached a point that we could occupy it without it being 100% complete. The connector has walls, roof, doors, windows, and is sealed enough that the A/C is working and the fire alarm system is operational. The plans are for the construction crews to work in the evenings on the connector until complete, while we have full access to the space during the school day …

The senior I ran into told me that the seniors should be allowed to put their handprints on the wall in the connector to show that they had some part and "connection" to the building project. What an awesome idea! Another senior chimed in to say that it was depressing to walk through the connector and it be in the unfinished condition that it was in (these seniors were told this past spring that they would be the first to use the new building!). I told these seniors that I would work on that idea …

By this afternoon and connecting to the two most senior-involved adults in the building, we came up with a plan for this to happen on Friday. My secretary would work on getting the supplies and a couple of adults to help "guide and facilitate" this process, and the senior guidance counselor and our college & career coach would communicate what we were doing among the seniors and the teachers (giving them a heads-up that seniors would be out of class for a short time to complete this project). The following was created and communicated by our CCR (College & Career Readiness) coach within 30 minutes of our impromptu meeting for this project that originated this morning in the mind of a senior:

WHEN: Friday, August 20, 2021
8:15-9:00 & 1:30-2:10

WHAT: Put your stamp on AHS - Come and
make your mark on the
NEW AHS addition!

WHERE: NEW AHS Connector

All supplies will be provided

Another "Dynamo" in action! …

<u>August 20, 2021</u> – BUSY day, today … I started in the teacher's eating area going through my special Friday breakfast routine (more on that later). I was joined by one of our "go-to" sub teachers who was a former teacher. We struck up a conversation about the sad politics behind the coronavirus and how much longer education would be working through these conditions. We both agreed that the lingering effect the coronavirus has had on society was completely unnecessary.

On this day, we had four substitute teachers covering for teachers who were out for different reasons (plus one permanent sub we have hired as a full-time employee at Apollo). ALL of these individuals were former teachers, each agreeing to put in a little "overtime" to continue supporting education.

The truth is ... if it weren't for these individuals, schools could not function on a day-to-day basis and would have to shut down. These individuals are our HEROES! Many of them have spent so many of the days at Apollo HS within the year, I am certain that there are students who think they are full-time employees!

The **_former_** governor of Kentucky had it **_all wrong_** when he publicly criticized educators for their banking of sick days and especially for the fact that these heroes "double-dip" (are receiving their retirement pay at the same time they are paid as a substitute teacher). WHO ELSE would you want covering for a regular teacher and give anything close to a day filled with quality instruction than a **_former teacher_**?? Can people off the streets fill these sub teaching positions and help carry on instruction when a teacher is out? Even IF they could, do these people even exist? In 32 years as an educator, I am only aware of one or two individuals who subbed that weren't former teachers. Quite frankly, those individuals weren't any good and were only used in an emergency.

The former governor did a lot of damage that created a fear among current educators, retired educators, and, especially, pre-educators because of his criticism and his efforts to change the retirement system and make it where you could not retire and return to substitute. In the last four years, the pipeline feeding the public education system has become a trickle, forcing some school districts to hire "Option 6" teachers (those with at least a BA but not certified as a teacher) to fill open positions or start the school year, shuffling subs into the open spots— many of which are not familiar with the subject that they are asked to teach. Yes, the pandemic has not helped the situation.

In Kentucky, at least, the "can-kicking", the criticisms educators have faced, and the pandemic have created a "perfect storm" that has crippled school systems to the point where we are right now. How much longer can education endure? ...

To continue this theme, giving attention to the lack of help that we have to function as a full staff at Apollo HS, I have spent my eighth day in a row as a cashier at lunch— we have been in school for eight days. One of our sub teachers was needed to cover one of our math teachers so that he could drive our FFA students to attend the state fair. The bus garage didn't have anyone who could drive our students, and our only means of making this happen was using the one teacher we have in the building who also has a CDL license. At the same time, we do not have adequate help in our front office to answer the phones, check students in and out, help any students or adults who stop by for assistance, etc. This has created a domino effect that pulls my secretary and the school's bookkeeper away from their normal duties ...

ON THE BRIGHT SIDE ... I do not want to leave the impression that it is ALL doom and gloom on days like today. We DID get to take our FFA students to the state fair— this is an opportunity that was taken away from them last year, and we made the commitment this year to do everything in our power to give our students these opportunities back (for as long as we can!). We also followed through with the "Put your stamp on AHS" activity today that we quickly put together in 48 hours. This activity was very uplifting to say the least. The seniors were all smiles and laughs, many of whom took a moment or two for a picture opportunity with their close friends. The many adults who pulled together to help with this event each left walking a few inches taller as well. THESE are the moments that we remember ...

Back to our heroes— THANK YOU for your dedication and your unwavering assistance during difficult times, helping us keep the doors of education open. We simply could NOT do this without you! ...

August 23, 2021 – Some Mondays are just that way ... As I entered my office to start the day, my secretary stopped by to tell me that the A/C was down in the 200 section of our building, 700 section, and the Media Center Area (brand- new system installed this summer!). She informed me that we had two of our three day custodians out today, but we had one of our evening custodians to come in and help out. This shortage of custodial work is troubling during normal times, but the fact that we cannot disinfect appropriately while this pandemic continues is alarming to say the least. The last two days of this past week we reported to our staff and families three and four positive cases respectively. Today, we had **_seven_** positive cases that warranted sending either students or staff home— also quarantining others.

———————— ◆ ————————

ENL (Eagles' Nest Live) is a media broadcast that is shown at the first 10 minutes of the school day. These students do a tremendous job covering announcements, and each student is also assigned to feature a "story" that is special for what is going on at the time. These students have a schedule for when their story will be featured and a very strict deadline to adhere to so that the editing and screening process will prevail. I have the pleasure of being a part of ENL on a daily basis. They typically end with me sharing anything special as far as announcements and giving the birthdays for the day.

Seeing these students in action, the pride that they each demonstrate in putting together their story or feature and the positive energy within the group and their teacher, MAKES MY DAY! It is an honor to be a part of this process, as ENL serves as the lifeblood that keeps the heart of Eagle Nation pumping at the very beginning of each day.

Last week, I made the comment that we were going to send a Google Poll to find out just how many people liked the "sporks" that the cafeteria was using. Since the start of the pandemic, our cafeteria has gone to disposable trays and utensils. Recently, they had traded out the plastic forks for sporks (all-in-one spoon/fork) and I mentioned on ENL how much I disliked them (adding a little fun and a lighter moment for my ENL time). I told the students that I would use my power and influence as a "Lunch Lady" to see if I can do anything about the sporks (very few people truly appreciate my humor!). Although I was just as serious at finding out how many approved of the sporks, I knew that the Google Poll would not produce the evidence or data I might have been looking for.

Since mentioning that on ENL, I have heard from two teachers who both expressed that they LOVE the sporks, and I also heard today from my buddy, "Darren". At the very beginning of his lunch period today (still at my cashier post), "Darren" walked up to me with a very serious look on his face and asked me how the poll was going. I asked him what his thoughts were on sporks; his response was, "It's the best thing that has EVER happened at Apollo HS!". This goes to show you that "Darren" doesn't require much to get him excited. After hearing this and realizing that staff and students seem to be firmly on one side of this debate or the other, I decided I need to send out a simple poll to see where Eagle Nation stands on ... yes, the topic of SPORKS! Details should be available to share later this week ...

———— ◆ ————

The evening custodian who came in to help this morning to get us through the day stopped by my office just after 2:00 to let me know that one of our evening custodians will no longer be with us. This individual just accepted a position at one of the district middle schools. He also reported that there were eleven custodians out throughout the eighteen schools in the district and that there are no subs for Apollo tonight. Because our one custodian left us, we had only one custodian left for the night crew with a new custodian (with limited English) starting tonight who needed to be shown around. Because this was the case, this dedicated evening custodian made the decision that he was going to stay the night and pull a back-to-back shift.

I immediately called the district custodial manager and asked what could be done to get us more help for the night. He mentioned that there were one or two other individuals who had been recently hired who would be starting later this week. I told him that this didn't help us tonight. He indicated that he did not know anything that could be done— all of the sub custodians are filling other positions throughout the district.

Poor soul— pulling a double shift, with another custodian not feeling 100%, and the only other help was from a new custodian (unfamiliar with the building) and limited communication! I told this **_very dedicated custodian_** to do the best that he could— that is all we could ask. I also sent out an email to all staff explaining that very little cleaning detail would be accomplished in classrooms this evening and that the three custodians in the building would be focused on halls, door handles, and restrooms.

On my drive home, I received a message from the Head Custodian for Apollo HS (one of the two day custodians who were out today) that indicated he'd tested positive for the coronavirus. What a day! ... Our custodial issues look to be getting substantially worse with him being out for a minimum of ten days. How many more custodians will leave? Will those recently hired stay? Some Mondays are just that way ...

August 24, 2021 – Tuesday of this week started with a meeting for our teacher interns in the World Language Dept. The state of Kentucky once had KTIP (Kentucky Teacher Intern Program) in place to help first-year teachers "learn the ropes" of education. As always happens, the state always thought highly of this program and it went through a few "renovations" until the state ran out of money for it. Naturally, the state turned the entire process over to the districts. Each district was basically responsible for implementing its own intern program.

We at Apollo HS feel strongly about the mentor experience and the multiple classroom observations supported with three cycle meetings and multiple means of feedback from the intern's mentor, the subject area specialist, and the principal. Therefore, from the time it was left up to us, we implemented the APOLLO Teacher Intern Program (ATIP).

For our meeting this morning, we met with our new Spanish Teacher Intern and Mentor as well as our new ASL Teacher and Mentor and went over the expectations of the program and the timelines for Cycles 1, 2, and 3. Unlike the KTIP program of old, which proved to be stressful on the intern with a crazy 3-ring binder portfolio expectation at the end of Cycle 3 (loaded with "evidence" from their teaching, planning, assessment, etc.), ATIP is very nurturing and supportive for the interns. We made that very clear with the interns before we dismissed— along with setting the official date of the Cycle 1 meeting so that we could all work back from that date and think of when we want to schedule our own observations.

This is one aspect of several that I am proud to have initiated as principal of Apollo HS. We even went so far as finding a way to provide a $1,000 stipend for each of the Mentors for their time outside the school day that they would be spending with the intern— not to mention the amount of time they would spend being "on call" if the intern ever needed anything. I simply cannot think of any other way that is a better support for first- year teachers than this type of experience. AND ... you might have guessed that our very own "dynamos" here at Apollo HS play KEY ROLES in this ATIP experience and providers of intern feedback on a regular basis! ...

———— ◆ ————

Channel 14 News (Evansville, Indiana) stopped by today to see me to discuss Apollo's Summer School success in recovering lost learning from the 2021 school year. This feat was accomplished by getting the teachers on board to plan instruction and teach students directly as opposed to signing the students up for the usual credit recovery software. The adults at Apollo realized that the most efficient way for us to get students to show us the skills they had missed out on was to work with them on main content and skills and assess them as if we were just extending the school year.

All of this sounds fair enough, but after the year that our teachers and students just went through, it was hard to imagine either side being able to put forth the required effort for this program to be successful. Quite frankly, the gas tanks were pretty empty for both staff and students at the end of May 2021.

Not that this would have made much of a difference, but we did manage to secure each teacher's daily wage threshold (DWT) for this special session of Summer School, instead of the usual $25- per- hour amount that teachers made throughout the year for ESS (Extended School Service). The teachers at Apollo HS would have rolled up their sleeves anyway and found a way to make the most of not one 2-week session for Summer School, but TWO 2-week sessions! The end result after four weeks of learning during the month of June (and a handful of students needing a little more time online in July) was 360 half-credits earned by our students! This would put our students in a much better setting to start the current year and many of them back on track to graduate with their peers.

I am **_extremely proud_** of this work by the twenty-eight (28) adults who made Summer School 2021 happen at Apollo HS, and I am thankful that the 300-plus students had the desire themselves and the support of their parents to attend. With the way this current year has started and the number of quarantines that have mounted up, we will likely be doing this again at the end of the year (HOPEFULLY, not at the same large scale). Yes, the pandemic continues to wreak havoc on our work ...

––––––––––– ◆ –––––––––––

This day ended with a little more drama than we like to expect. For one, two Daviess County sheriff's deputies showed up to process some information that was shared by one of our students. A sexual assault took place a year ago and not even on campus, but the Apollo student had information that needed to be shared. To get through this inquisition, one of our assistant principals made for a good sounding board for our student (this is a GOOD problem to have— the **_only_** way that we can support finding the help that our students need!).

We also had another stand by our female student who refused to wear a mask in one of her classes. Today, she was able to garner the support of a close friend to take the same stand with her. As the dean of students escorted the young ladies to his office, the same "f@#k the world" mother was on her way to pick up her daughter. As you may have guessed, mom was wearing the SAME t-shirt today!

The mother was clearly reacting to our governor rescinding his face-mask executive order yesterday— this is the same executive order that started the first conversation with FTW mom. Little did FTW mom know that the Kentucky Board of Ed. and Kentucky Dept. of Ed. released a statement not long after the governor's statement to say that the Kentucky mask mandate was still on, according to the direction that they had given all school districts. The word "ignorant" comes to mind here which most people would take high offense to, but it simply is a reference to this mother **_lacking knowledge or awareness_** *in general*. We seem to be dealing with this more frequently nowadays than we have in the past ...

It's approaching 7:00 pm— off to our home VB contest with our close city rival ... Home late tonight! ... 10:30 to be exact! ...

August 26, 2021 (LOCKDOWN!! This is NOT a drill! ...) – This is the one event that we all drill for but hope never happens. We always hear about it happening at other schools, but never at OUR school ...

At 8:03 this morning, one of our assistant principals got on the radio and asked me to call a Lockdown. There was no detail given with this call, but I could hear the urgency in his voice. Thankfully, I was **very** near the PA system and within seconds made the announcement, "LOCKDOWN! ... We need a LOCKDOWN. Get everyone to a safe location or classroom. LOCKDOWN! ... This is NOT A DRILL ... LOCKDOWN!!" The office personnel were swiftly moving students to the safety of the back offices. Students were flying by the office trying to get to the closest classroom. [REPEAT Announcement to reinforce what was happening.] I was barking a few orders for staff to contact the Board Office to share what was going on; at the same time, I could hear on the radio the assistant principals and our school law- enforcement officer communicating who they were trying to find and where he might be.

Considering that we made the lockdown announcement seven minutes before the school day officially started, our students and staff performed remarkably well and had everyone safe within a couple of LONG minutes. It wasn't long after securing students that I heard over the radio that the suspect the administrators were looking for had been detained and put in custody by our school law- enforcement officer. No shots fired; nobody brandishing a weapon; and, no direct threat to any student. This is EXACTLY what you practice for, and we HOPE that it unfolds as I have described if the actual event were to happen.

Knowing that we had the situation in control and especially that every-one was safe, I went to my secretary to prepare our first message to go out to parents. By this time, our superintendent and our Director of Pupil Personnel (DPP) were on site and in the office. We quickly de-vised a plan for what we could share. The most important information to get out quickly was to acknowledge that a Lockdown was called, the students were safe, and the situation was "contained". At 8:19 am, this message was sent out with my voice speaking directly to our parents and families: "We will keep you posted as we have more information to share ..."

In the meantime, we still had all staff and students locked in rooms, lights out, and VERY anxious as to what had happened— what was go-ing on? The entire building outside our office was SILENT.

Once we had the student in custody and the BB gun that looked EXACTLY like a .40-caliber pistol in our possession, I asked for con-firmation that we had enough information to know this one student was acting alone. Once this was confirmed, I knew that we had to give the "all-clear". Unfortunately, it is not as easy as getting on the PA and announcing "all-clear". Our teachers are trained to know that each room must be unlocked and cleared by an administrator or law- en-forcement officer. The problem was, all the law- enforcement officers on site were working to gather information and put pieces together to find out what caused this student to make the choice he did to bring a weapon to school. This takes time and plenty of note-taking. Two of our assistant principals were helping with this process because they knew the student and could help give information of events that had happened earlier this week.

It is a tedious and painstaking process for one or two people to try to unlock every classroom door in the building. I helped with this for some of the closest classrooms to the office, fumbling each time with the lock. In our old building, it seems that ***every door*** has its own trick to unlock. I continued this until I realized that there was nobody back in the office to answer questions or to make decisions needed moving forward. Based on this, I went back to the office and waited to hear on the radio what the progress was on getting the rooms all-clear.

In the meantime, parents were outside the building wanting to pick up their students. We had to get them some information and explain that we HAD to take attendance to see who was in the building. We had to get our students to their 1st- period class (several of our students had gone to the closest classroom) and take accurate attendance in Infinite Campus ("IC" — our student information system), THEN allow for students to be picked up by a parent and ONLY if the parent showed up in person with their driver's license.

In these scenarios, parents can be your worst enemy. We completely understand that they want to find out if their child is OK, even though this situation was quickly contained and nobody was harmed. The problem is, in the early stages of this event, the parents were "in the way" and eating up some time that we needed to be spending clearing classrooms and ensuring our staff that the building was safe. We also needed to inform them what we needed next. Because students were texting their parents within seconds of the Lockdown announcement, some of them arrived at school within ten minutes and before the Daviess County deputies responded. They stood at our locked front doors expecting to be picking up their children. At that point, again, we hadn't even taken attendance for the day to even know who was actually present.

While we were preparing a written statement to be handed out to our growing number of parents at the front doors, our teachers and students were still waiting to receive information that everything was OK. It is heartbreaking to think of our students and our staff in that very anxious and emotional position that they were in.

Before we even had a chance to get the facts out to our community for what took place (BB gun that looked real, suspect in custody within minutes, nobody harmed), social media and the "fire-starters" had already taken over. Shots were fired; multiple gunmen, school resource officer shot and in critical condition. Holding this information at bay or making any effort to get out AHEAD of this misinformation is FUTILE in the days of social media. At the point that you just mention "lockdown has occurred ... weapon" to our parents, you may as well prepare for the students to be picked up. Many of our parents were adding fuel to the "fire" that had been started and some were criticizing our reaction. A few even went so far as accusing Apollo of "covering it all up". In this day and time, especially after very public events that have happened across our nation these past couple of years, it has reached a point that people just believe what they want to believe.

Because the parent pick-up line had grown and extended far onto the neighboring streets, we did our best to process the check out quickly. There were a minimum of five adults on the phones and at the front desk to help expedite this. While this checkout process was going on, we could NOT dismiss our students from 1st period (normally 1st period ends at 9:08). If we had made ANY class change at all while parents were checking students out, we would have lost several of them to other exits. How embarrassing would it be if Joey Smith's parent had arrived to pick him up and Joey wasn't in his 2nd period class? This would have caused even more panic and fuel to the already blazing fire. As a school, we had to hold firm on the decision we made to stay in 1st period, despite the encouragement of the Board Office staff to move on to a normal day.

We remained in 1st period until around 12:45, which means we had to devise a plan to allow each room to take their students to the cafeteria to get their lunch and then return to eat their lunch in the classroom. This was organized and facilitated by none other than our "Dynamos" that I have mentioned previously ...

We ended the day with a special-called faculty meeting so that we could fully inform our staff to make sure they knew everything that had happened this morning. We wanted to make sure that they all understood that the students involved were apprehended swiftly and that nobody was hurt. The LAST thing you ever want is for the staff to find out from the newspaper details that the administration had failed to share. I also wanted to take the opportunity to THANK every one of them for their response and for getting students to safety so quickly, considering again that the call for lockdown came before the school day began. They ALL did a phenomenal job, and many of them stepped up and helped us manage the details that followed (student check outs, etc.) without us asking for help.

We gave the staff the timeline of events and made sure they were aware that the TWO students who had brought weapons to school were both charged and escorted out of the building, likely to never see the inside of Apollo HS again. We gave the staff an opportunity to ask questions and also warned them that there were already several exaggerated details being shared on social media— to include that there were "shots fired" and Officer Klee had been shot in the leg and was in critical condition. We needed help from our staff to get help dispelling the rumors—at the VERY least, confirm that when they hear the exaggerated details they acknowledge that THOSE details WERE NOT TRUE. The staff seemed to recognize this and understand.

The last item we shared was details for how we would have a Social-Emotional Learning (SEL) discussion about the event just after ENL on Friday morning. I would explain the same timeline to the students and make sure that they knew the TRUTH as to what took place this morning. Our Lead Guidance Counselor (Apollo Grad!) would be on ENL to explain to the students what HIS experience was during the lockdown (in a dark, locked room for a seemingly LONG time) and also follow up explaining the SEL discussion that we would have about the lockdown experience. The staff had just a couple of questions and then we dismissed. What a mentally and physically **_exhausting_** day! ...

Official student attendance: 88.5%.

August 27, 2021 (Day after Lockdown) – I was very curious how many of our students would return today after Thursday's traumatic event. The day started with seemingly the normal number of students walking the halls and in the Commons Area before school. The faces that I ran into were smiling (behind masks, of course) and responding to my "Good Morning", for the most part. Adults I ran into seemed to be in a good place. We had a follow-up faculty meeting for those who had small children to pick up or appointments the day before. In this meeting, some emotions came out indicating that some of our teachers had triggered some trauma from the past having gone through the anxious moments of our lockdown (not knowing that everything was OK). This teacher had every reason to relive the grief that she experienced and I felt guilty that I had not focused more on communicating to our teachers and staff than to pacify the parents waiting at our front doors. This is something I have committed to change if this event ever happens again (praying that it doesn't!) ...

The ENL broadcast seemed to be a powerful and uplifting moment, and the follow-up with the teachers during 1st period seemed to go well with teachers moving on to some form of instruction within 10 minutes. This was very relieving considering the anxiety that all had experienced the day before. We had a "special" Leadership Team Meeting (**always** one on Fridays at 8:30 am) for the purpose of going over the procedures we followed for the lockdown and what needed to be changed/improved upon. One of the items I asked for was to be sure that my secretary and I would be available strictly to keep the communication flowing. The Board Office personnel who always join us in the event of an emergency can be the ones to be the "messenger" for our parents. Overall, this was a good meeting and we came up with a few suggestions to make the next emergency a little more strategic.

The rest of the school day was uplifting as I interacted as much as I could with staff and students. I, once again, took up my spot as one of the cashiers for lunch, and this gave me an opportunity for "Thank you" (for having their ID ready for scanning) and "Have a nice weekend." It is good to hear from the students returning the greetings. This is EXACTLY what I needed after the day we had yesterday! ...

The only other thing that we experienced throughout the day was the concern from different students and even some staff that they'd "heard" that there was going to be "violence" or "gangs with guns" at our first home football game that we had with one of our inner-city rivals. EVERY lead was followed, but it could never be traced back to a source giving us any detailed information to even look up. No names involved in the "violence" and no original source for the "rumors" floating around. We attributed what was going around as a "spillover" reaction to what had taken place the day before with a "gun" (albeit BB gun) on campus with a full-fledged lockdown. Our reaction was to ensure we had extra security in the form of Daviess County sheriff's deputies along with DCPS officers on hand. Normally, we have 6 for these types of games. Tonight we will have 10— closely monitoring at the gates for entry, throughout the game, and the parking lot after the game ...

86.6% was the official attendance for the day.

————— ♦ —————

The game went off without a hitch; HUGE crowd. An excellent weather night for late August and not too humid. The worst part was that our rival was having their way with us in the first half. 34 to 0 at halftime! The second half went much quicker (running clock), and the game finally came to an end with a 44 to 7 Apollo loss.

As I made my way to my vehicle after the game, I could hear the chatter starting to pick up on our security radios (every admin and every officer had one). "We need back up in the parking lot, we have something going on!" I drove to the location a lot quicker than I could have on foot to find that the officers had two "assailants" on the ground and in cuffs and one victim in the back of a car. Several onlookers were taking their time passing by as they left the game. It wasn't long before Apollo's school officer was seen making his way back to the "crime scene" with a third "assailant " who had fled through the nearby soybean field.

After hanging around long enough to start putting the pieces together as to what had happened, I realized that ***a shot had been fired*** and that two of the attackers were armed. Nobody was hurt except for the attacker, who had actually shot himself in the leg trying to get to his gun during the skirmish. It turns out that this attack had nothing at all to do with Apollo HS and nothing really related to our opponent. This attack was the result of retaliation from a shooting that had taken place downtown earlier in the week. Three cousins, potentially associated with the same gang, had targeted this other individual on his way out of the stadium.

After ALL of the anxiety from the lockdown the day before, after ALL of the "chatter" that was going around from different people at school about "violence" or "someone is bringing a gun" that we could not trace, this was the LAST thing Apollo HS needed. Again, we were so fortunate that nobody within Apollo was hurt, but our people have been given more evidence to consider that maybe Apollo isn't so safe after all?

The administrators and I left Apollo's parking lot sometime after 11:00 pm. I had sent all Apollo staff an email just to inform them that NOBODY from Apollo was involved and that this incident had nothing to do with lockdown on Thursday.

———— • ————

I slept well Friday night into Saturday morning, but only because I was exhausted from the previous day's events. My mind was racing most of the weekend. How would our public receive this information? If we felt that our attendance at school was bad Friday, how good did we expect our attendance to be Monday morning?

On Sunday, I sent a calendar invite to our Leadership Team to prepare them for a meeting at 9:30 am Monday. My ask for them was to think of ways we could get our students back into our building AND the trust from our parents to ensure the safety of their children. Today's society and the conditions we have all lived through these past two years especially, very few people trust authority. If the superintendent or the principal of a building are not the ones who are listened to (by students OR parents), WHO could be called upon to deliver the message about the safety and conditions of Apollo ***that would be heard***? ...

Monday, August 30, 2021 – Students and staff were nervous on Monday morning, but I was also surprised and relieved to see smiles and cheerful voices in the crowd. If our attendance was going to be any indication of the numbers we saw before school started, it wasn't going to be as bad as I had imagined. Still, we heard the rumor that "someone said there was a bomb" that quickly led to a source at a nearby school who had created a fake account to spread even more fear and make it look like someone else. This young man was about to be charged with terroristic threatening.

One of our 9th- grade students had called his mother prior to the beginning of school, nervous and fearful for all the things being dis-cussed around him. His mother naturally called the school to find out what was going on and asked for us to talk to her son. I called him to the office and proceeded to find out what the cause was for his con-cern. After speaking with this young freshman, I could tell that he had overheard "someone talking about a bomb". With his senses on "high alert" from the events that ended our week, this is only natural. My secretary and I assured him that our officers had checked all leads on this information and that he did the right thing to share the informa-tion. We did ask that he bring this information to us FIRST in the future in the case that there might be something to what he heard.

For this morning, just like Friday morning, we had increased DCPS security so that we would have more of a "secure" entrance— again, just as a precaution. We had a couple of students that we needed to collect for questioning (that **could have been** related to Thursday's events). These students were not here at the end of last week, but we feel that could have been a result of some of the related drama. We wanted to be sure to speak with them first. Because not all of the of-ficers here this morning knew our students, we had printed pictures of the students we wanted to find.

Seeing officers with the pictures of the students made one of our se-nior female students nervous, thinking "something was going down", so she called her mother to pick her up. School had not quite started yet. Mother demanded to speak with me and ask why we didn't do a better job checking the "backgrounds" of students before we allow them entry and enrollment in our schools. This is one of those "lose-lose" conversations with a naive and irrational parent who doesn't realize the rights of JUVENILE students and EVERY student's right to a FREE and appropriate public education. Before mother left after talking to me and our DPP for the district, she mentioned that she felt she needed to *home- school* her daughter if we couldn't be any more protection for her (too many "rapists" and "criminals" in our school— we were not even sure what she was referring to). I asked the mother, "Does your daughter plan to go to college?" Mother said "yes," and in that moment I felt she got my point. I further explained that isolation from the rest of her daughter's high school experience is NOT the answer to preparing her for what she will be facing in college and on her own the rest of her life. Mother left, very disheartened about what she was hearing and uncertain about what to do next.

The rest of the morning was uneventful, leading up to our 9:30 am Special-Called Leadership Team Meeting. Once gathered, I feel that the team could sense the tension and concern I was emitting. 86.6% attendance on Friday— ***before*** the violence at the ball game. My question posed to the group was what we could do to gain the trust of our families to secure the safety of their children and get these students back in school? I told the team that I felt this was far too important to just let happen and hope for the best. I felt that we needed to do something. Any ideas? ...

Crickets .... That is a deafening sound to hear at moments that you feel you are at the end of your rope. The only idea that was offered was to continue doing something that we were already doing. Not good enough— keep thinking. Our Lead Guidance Counselor mentioned that we need to be more intentional about making contacts with students and staff before school and between classes. When they see us and interact with us, they have a better feeling that "everything is OK". Getting better, KEEP THINKING.

The question I posed over the weekend is where we settled as we ended our short meeting. We agreed on the 6 to 8 most beloved and trusted adults at Apollo HS that have the most respect and are popular among students and parents alike. THESE adults would work together to craft a message that "APOLLO IS SAFE" and we would like to have your students back in school for the opportunity to TEACH THEM and prepare them for their future success ... You know, like the "old days" before violence and the coronavirus got in the way!

The rest of the day seemed semi-normal as I cashiered at lunch and interacted with the students and lunch ladies. After EVERYTHING we have been through, this is an absolute PURE JOY that provides some soup for the soul!

I also had my FIRST opportunity to visit a classroom for the year! Shamefully, yes, the 14th day of the school year, I finally have time to stop by for a quick classroom visit (10 to 12 minutes). The classroom I chose couldn't have been a better choice to pick me up at the end of the day. In her self-reflection to start the year, this teacher had commented how one of her classes brought her the most challenge because of the "energy" among the students. Even with two other adults in the room (Co-teacher and DHH Interpreter), it was hard to establish a rapport with the students in the early days of the year and channel their energy for the good of the classroom. At the end of the day, this teacher found herself EXHAUSTED! ...

As luck would have it, THIS was the class I was walking into. The teacher was going over a review with the students over a short story they were reading, and her method was a rapid-fire approach, pulling an index card with the name of the student that she was going to call on. She must have selected THE perfect short story for them to read because nearly every hand was going up and the students attached to those hands were pleading for the teacher to call on them.

Are you kidding me?? The rapport and respect displayed in this room as the teacher and co-teacher channeled the energy guiding the students into the proper protocol of not blurting out answers. Whatever work this teacher had employed from the time that she had written her self-reflection until now was PAYING OFF! I have witnessed this teacher in her element before— no matter the level of challenge in her students, she *always* seems to find a way to have them eating out of her hand. What I observed was no set up, no "dog-n-pony" act. There was no way for her to know I would be popping in on my way back to the office from talking to a nearby teacher. This visit made my day! ...

85.6% attendance today— not as bad as I had expected, but STILL nowhere near what it needs to be for us to fully function as a public high school ...

September 1, 2021 – This was the first day of the ENL Special Broadcast of the Apollo teachers having a conversation about the lockdown last Thursday and how they had personally processed the event as well as their own personal experience at the time the lockdown had been called. The three teachers sat and talked with each other while being recorded via video. They each took turns asking a question while the other two answered from their experience. This was just what the doctor ordered! The teachers were all "rock stars" in the eyes of the students and the other teachers in the building. Each one talked about the vulnerable moment that they all had with the lockdown, made it personal, and expressed to EVERY person viewing that THEY WERE

HUMAN. By the time that the video was done, the teachers confirmed that it was "OK to be scared" — the most important thing was that they were all SAFE ...

This made my day! I am hoping that the other staff and especially the students in our building received the message the same way that it was intended. Hopefully this will ease some of the drama, angst, and fear that came from the two events that happened at our school last week. Both unrelated and nothing to do with any REAL threat to Apollo students and staff.

The rest of the day went "normal" with me playing my role as a cashier at lunch, as I have done every day before (except the lockdown day). We have added our Athletic Director as a cashier as well at the other end of the lunch lines (there are a total of five serving lines that add to the variety that the cafeteria staff offers our students at Apollo HS). He has not served as a cashier every day like I have, but there have been several days he has been needed so far ... again, because we have not been able to hire all of the cafeteria staff that we need to fully function (typically, 16 cafeteria staff members serve Apollo HS).

The attendance today was 88.5%. Still abysmal— something is going to have to change and soon ...

September 2, 2021 – Thursday started out as a busy day with impromptu meetings along with scheduled meetings. I had gathered a portion of the leadership at our new "connector" to show them the idea I had for adding bistro tables and bar stools in what would be known as the "Senior Corner". This is where our seniors had all left their handprint a couple of weeks ago. This space was a "gift" and not one we saw being usable while looking at the floor plans. It is areas like this that you don't realize have potential for use until the construction happens.

I gave this small team my vision for what this area would be used for, the type of furniture to purchase, and where the money would come from. They would be responsible to take this little project from there. To be honest, these are the projects that I have always enjoyed in the past and would eagerly take the reins and see through to the very end. Knowing that my retirement is near, I feel it is better that the people who will be here much longer than I make these types of decisions. Also, I always lean towards a more traditional style of furniture, where others may look at a more modern approach. Bottom line: better to make those who will be walking by this area much longer than I be responsible for what it should look like.

During lunch today, one connection I have made EVERY day is with one of our EL (English Language) students, "Terpan". He had the very same ritual every single day. He always waited until the last person went through the line to come up and get his lunch. He always chose the pizza, pasta, or Mexican line no matter what was being served in the other lines.

"Terpan" is on our boys' soccer team and I remember him well from past years. He is very quiet and reserved, but responds well when someone takes an interest in him and what he is doing. I have made a point to go ahead and look him up as he is getting his lunch and make an exaggerated "Ole" gesture as he walks by my register without having to scan his ID (it really does not matter what he gets, as all school lunches for students are free again this year due to the pandemic). Today, he is wearing his soccer jersey, which indicates we have a game. "I've got you, Terpan! Good luck tonight, buddy! Score a goal for me!" "Terpan's" response is always the same— a HUGE smile and "Thank you".

The rest of the day was just as busy and over before I could get much completed (moving from conversation or meeting to the next). Attendance today is still not much better: 88.7% ...

———— ◆ ————

The best part of the day? "Terpan" scores the ONLY goal in the soccer game to give Apollo HS Boys the win!!

September 3, 2021 – Friday before Labor Day Weekend! This is a day that ALWAYS puts the students and staff in a good mood, everyone asking each other what their plans are for the next three days. This Friday proved to be even busier for me than the day before.

We always start off our Fridays with a Leadership Team Meeting. This group is comprised of all administrators, Dean of Students, Lead Guidance Counselor, two instructional coaches (aka "Dynamos"), College & Career Readiness Coach, Athletic Director, and my personal secretary. We always have a short agenda of four to five items that is generated by me or anyone else needing to bring an item to the group. We also always finish by looking into the next week for the special events and the athletic contests that will require administrator presence. The first item on the agenda was ATTENDANCE.

My point to the team was that we had to initiate something in order to get our students back in the building— we could not just wait for something to happen and the attendance get better on its own. With 88% attendance and around 4% of our students quarantined (not counted in our absence calculation), this means that 84% of our student body is walking the halls of Apollo HS. This is not enough for us to fully function as a high school and have successful results for learning and earning credits. I proposed that we take a look at the students who were absent this week and take a look at reasons for absence. We also need to identify our chronic absence students and get some help from the Central Office and the Student Services personnel to get some intervention meetings started.

The assistant principal in charge of attendance communicated that they were already tracking this and had a list generated with details for contacts that had been made along with home visits. I asked the assistant principal to share this list with me. One of our instructional coaches asked if other schools were experiencing the same attendance issues, or if it was just Apollo. Good question! I made a note to find out, but I expressed that we really need to make an effort to improve our attendance regardless.

This day continued at a rapid pace with my usual stop in principal duties for 90 minutes of cashiering at the lunch line. Imagine how pressed you would be to complete your normal duties if you had an hour and a half EVERY day blocked out of your schedule. Again, I certainly enjoy connecting with the students, but it takes a toll on my ability to keep up, and there are days it wears me out. Some of these days warrant a power nap as soon as I get home ...

At the beginning of our last period of the day, we always have afternoon announcements. Sometimes, these announcements are a repeat of the AM announcements, but it also allows me to send a message or express best wishes for our teams who will be competing. I don't always make announcements (most of the time our front desk secretary takes care of this), but on this day I decided to wish everyone a SAFE and HEALTHY Labor Day weekend. To our faculty and staff, I told them all to take time to "find their Lake Cumberland".

This is an expression that I started at the beginning of last year when

I shared the experience of my family and I during the summer of 2020 on our first of what became an annual trip to Lake Cumberland for a long weekend. With Covid-19 and the pandemic ramping up, this was the perfect getaway for us. My wife, Angela, and I have four children, and three of them are off on their own. It is rare that we are all together enjoying each other's company (only the major holidays), and the pandemic had made it even more infrequent. With our cabin- at-the- lake experience, we didn't have to see anyone else or do anything but enjoy the outdoors and the pleasure of relaxing with each other. At the start of last school year, knowing that it was going to be a difficult year (starting out in "Red Status" with 0 students in the building), I encouraged our staff to look out for each other and to take care of ourselves by taking every moment that we could to "find our Lake Cumberland". This message became our mantra as we navigated through the most difficult year that any of us had …

Not long after the announcements, I had a visit from our new ASL (American Sign Language) teacher. We took advantage of the fact that our French teacher retired after being with us for three years AND the fact that Kentucky was now accepting ASL as a foreign language credit to start offering two class periods of ASL 1. This teacher is a blessing to Apollo HS. She is the mother of a recent Apollo graduate and also of twin freshman girls who are members of the E-gals Volleyball Team. She is deaf and has to use ASL to formally communicate herself. Because I know very little sign (but, I am learning!), I always get out a small legal pad for her to write down what she wants to say:

Nikki Boarman got accepted to Eastern KY U!

I am happy!

Kids love the class!

They tell me "I Love You" in sign!

I thought you would want to know …

Between each of her statements, I acknowledged what she had written by signing "YES!" as an indication that I had heard the good news. I also held my hands over my heart to indicate that her news made my heart feel good! I signed "thank you!" at the end of her written expression, I finished by writing, "Have a **good** weekend!" She signed "you too" as she turned to leave …

What a way to finish this week going into the holiday weekend! This was the highlight of my day for sure! On the not- so- bright side, we finished our week averaging 87.9% attendance, and we found that our rival high school across town had averaged 92.9%. This makes our attendance situation more dire … We have our work cut out for us! …

September 7, 2021 —- What a beautiful weekend! If any of our staff was not able to "find their Lake Cumberland" these past three days, it certainly was not because the weather wouldn't allow it. Personally, I took full advantage of the weather and spent some time on the road driving through Small Town America in southern Indiana. It was good to come back to work today and have follow-up conversations with each adult and some of the students, asking if they enjoyed their three-day weekend. It is always fulfilling to hear the good things that others are involved in and that they enjoyed themselves. This is good therapy for ANYONE involved in these conversations. Now, it is "back to the grind" …

My secretary and I reserved some good news that all staff would appreciate hearing for this morning. We had the pleasure of having one of our teachers announced as the DCPS High School Teacher of the Year at the Opening Day Celebration before our school year began. As an honor to the school and the teacher, our district office sends $1,000 to be spent as "we" see fit— either on classroom materials OR it could be spent on a reception in honor of the recipient. Between this teacher and me, we felt it was a perfect opportunity to reward the entire staff by paying for everyone's lunch via our favorite food truck (Real Hacienda!).

To help expedite everyone's order, my secretary came up with a Google Form that would take down everyone's order of choice, their name, and what lunch shift they had (1st, 2nd, or 3rd). The Real Hacienda staff would be on site from 11:00 to 1:00 and would know the order to start preparing the meals and have staff member names on the Styrofoam container and ready to go so the adults would not have to wait in line. With only 30 minutes allowed per lunch shift, we knew that several would not be able to make an order at the window, wait, and have enough time to eat it before they had to go back to class. This new procedure would be a tremendous help that would allow anyone who wanted a FREE Real Hacienda lunch to participate.

I sent this Google Form link in an email this morning, explaining the details for WHY we had this opportunity and HOW it would work. The response was instantaneous with several personal thank- yous that followed. I told my secretary that this would be the FIRST deadline that we have EVER established that is met by 100% of our adults! Chuckle, yes, but SADLY true!

The past two years with educators working in the pandemic conditions that we have all been forced in, I have made it a part of my Professional Growth Plan (PGP) as principal to keep a pulse on the culture/climate of the school and go so far as ensuring that our staff members remained "in a good place" (both mentally and physically). To do this, I have stopped and talked to teachers while they are on planning period or in passing; I have also spoken with staff members, just to see how they and their family members have been doing. This past year with many of our school days WITHOUT students in our building, we set up the occasional food truck to stop by for lunch. Some days the staff members purchased their own. A handful of Food Truck days were paid for by the school (using appropriate funds, of course!). The staff thoroughly enjoyed these opportunities (paid for or not) and it made for good de-escalation or bonding moments for our teachers/staff to connect and check in with each other while they were waiting in line for their orders to be expedited.

It took a lot of careful and creative planning of as many "feel- good moments" for our staff to get through THE most challenging year ever recorded for education. Thanks to the help from our office staff, my now-retired secretary, and our Culture/Climate Committee, we were able to have as many of these events planned to effectively keep our staff in the right place. At least, I THINK(?).

Another one of my goals as the principal of Apollo was to make certain that we did not lose any of our good teachers to retirement or resignation due to the working conditions. Sadly, I know of two phenomenal educators that I strongly feel would NOT have retired and still would likely be working if the conditions were "normal" (at least as " normal" as things were prior to the pandemic [Fall 2019]). We had nine teachers/staff members retire or move on to bigger/better opportunities at the end of last year. On average, this is more than what we typically have had at Apollo HS. Are you ready for this? I have told others that this number will GREATLY increase at the end of this current year. With each day that passes and educators having to work in conditions making their jobs doubly hard, this is guaranteed. For the future of education, I hope and pray that I am wrong ...

Extra pay or the promise of supplemental pay will make no difference at this point. For many of us, our "cans" have simply been kicked down the road for far too long …

88.3% attendance today.

September 9, 2021 – Very few things hit a school, its staff, and students as hard as the death of a current student. It has only happened once before in my 31- year career. There have been several recently graduated students, but only one current student that I have had—that is, until today …

Just two short weeks ago, Apollo HS experienced the traumatic lockdown. This passing of a student is another event that Apollo HS staff and students have experienced that will send some on an emotional roller-coaster ride. Although every one of our students was caught off-guard today in receiving this news, the administrators, counselors, and teachers closest to this student have been preparing themselves for this moment. When we received the news just before the school day began, it still hurt and once again felt like we had been hit by a ton of bricks …

No matter how much it hurt, we had to maintain our composure for our students. More importantly, we had to prepare for communication to go out in a timely fashion. Some of our students in the building were related to this student and they had no knowledge of this student's passing when they arrived at school today. This complicated things a great deal. We had to work with our District Crisis Team to prepare some personal communications to go to individual students and their families. We also wanted to be sure to communicate to students who were close from the previous graduating class. Because of the nature of this student who passed, this was critically important.

We also had the obligation to inform the rest of our student body today, in a formal fashion by holding a moment of silence, and be sure we did this at least two hours before the end of the day so that the students had time to process the information and seek individual counseling if it was needed. This was a lot to take on and communicate to each stakeholder group BEFORE this became another social- media fire that burns out of control. All it takes is ONE spark, and the LAST thing we want to happen in cases like this is for our staff, our students, and our community to be misinformed and hear it through social media …

In times like this, I thank my lucky stars for the district public relations specialist and that DCPS is a large enough district to have one. This individual has been a rock-solid supporter for me and everything Apollo HS in times that we have needed communication. When my attention as principal is needed elsewhere, this individual has always been there and has provided the template of communication that the school has needed. The best part of this support has been the mutual respect that we both have shared for making the communications to Apollo genuine. She has always steered me in the "proper" things to say or the proper ways to say it. I have always put the Apollo "twist" that needed to be said. In the end, we respect that each has contributed to the communication.

This PR person was prepared to help us communicate what was needed. The three teachers closest to the student who passed, our lead guidance counselor, and the Crisis Team worked to see that the communication to our parents was right— the PR specialist made sure to pick up the communication that needed to go out to the public. I went into "leader-mode" and offered a timeline of communication that we HAD to adhere to in order to communicate to ALL that needed direct communication, while respecting and honoring our student with a moment of silence before the end of the day. The following timeline was what I challenged our team with:

- I would send a "DO NOT SHARE" email to all staff at Apollo at 9:00 am to inform them of the passing of the student. I did not want to catch them by surprise by sharing the news with them at the same time we did the students. Most of the teachers in the building were preparing themselves, just as the guidance and administrators had. I also wanted to make them aware we had to inform **_certain students in our building who did not know_** and also allow time enough for close family to be informed.

- From 9:00 until roughly 12:30, we had to inform INDIVIDUALS whom we felt needed this courtesy. This included the 30 families whose children were closest to this student and the option for those students to go home and receive the news from their parents. Our three teachers each started making phone calls to meet this deadline.

- At 1:00 or so, the current students who were classmates of this student would be informed by the three teachers.

- At 1:25 (the start of 5th period), IF all previous timelines and tasks had been met, we would make the PA announcement, honor our student with a moment of silence, and offer our students the opportunity for counseling.

- At 2:00, our special communication to all families would go out. We would send a message to say that "you may want to be prepared to talk to your child when they get home". These mass communications always go out by TEXT, saying, "Please be prepared to check your email for important communication from the principal of Apollo HS". The special letter is attached to the email.

This challenge that I presented to the team was certainly a steep hill to climb, but our team did it ... and in Apollo "Eagle Family" fashion.

After making the announcement to the school over the PA (one of the more difficult announcements I have EVER made), I took a moment to watch the bank of TV monitors that make up our camera security system throughout the building. I did this to see if there was any reaction in any area of the building, and also gave it a moment to see if there was any movement towards our guidance offices. Every scene that I watched from many angles throughout our campus was peaceful ...

I paused long enough to make sure that students had the opportunity to process what they had heard and seek individual counseling if that is what they needed, and later headed to the Guidance Office area. As I passed our lead guidance counselor's office, I noticed my good friend "Darren" talking to him; at the same time, he noticed me walking by the office. "Darren" sprang up from his chair and opened the door to see me. He was trying to talk through his emotions and embrace me at the same time. I heard what he had to say and I coaxed him to come back into the counselor's office where the three of us could continue the conversation.

Poor "Darren" — he had connections to the young man who made the poor decision to bring the BB gun two weeks ago, and he had connections to the student who had passed away. As I listened in on the conversation between our lead counselor and "Darren", I thought about how ironic this was and the fact that something was always bringing "Darren" and I together at the times that Apollo HS was experiencing the most difficult challenges. There are roughly 1,480 students at Apollo HS this year, and "Darren" and I seemed to have some kind of bond that brought the two of us near each other on several occasions. Although I could not imagine what "Darren" was going through being closely tied to both individuals in this short amount of time, I realized that it was my connection to "Darren" that provided me strength to get through these moments.

As our conversation ended and we felt better about "Darren" being in a "good place", I went back to the office to check to see if any calls had been made in regards to the special communication sent at 2:00 pm. A handful of calls HAD been made and, thankfully, ALL in support of what the Eagle Family was going through. I went to my office to close out this emotionally draining day …

89.5% attendance today …

September 10, 2021 – Tomorrow marks the 20th anniversary of 9/11. It is hard to believe that it has been twenty years since that disastrous day, and even harder to believe that none of our students were even thought of when that event took place. Most of our seniors were born in 2004. To bring awareness to this moment in the history of our country, we prepared a special video that was made of live clips from the newscast on 9/11 and the four airliners that crashed. As a lead-in for this video, one of our social studies teachers introduced the topic and also shared his "I'll always remember what I was doing …" with the students. The video was a perfect representation of what happened. It took EVERY one of us adults back to that fateful day …

As a follow-up, I thanked the ENL cast and the social studies teacher for making this memorial happen, and I encouraged the students to think of ways they could be a part of the GOOD that exists in this world. There is far too much hate, and it is hate that ultimately leads to unfortunate disasters like 9/11.

It was also important for us to call attention to the death of our student and the love and support needed for the family to get through this difficult time. This family is one who adopts children, and they would have a hard time affording the funeral costs and medical costs. I mentioned that the funeral arrangements would be shared as soon as we knew them, and we would also let everyone know the details of any collection that we would be taking up to support the family.

What a somber morning— it makes it hard to focus on our work and move forward, but it is exactly what we witnessed among the adults and students in the building today.

It was a busy morning with the usual Friday leadership team meeting, and that meeting led up to a district secondary principals' meeting at the Board Office. By the time I got to the Board Office, my mind was a million miles away due to a threat that had been made indicating violence at our second home football game tonight … ARE YOU KIDDING ME?!?! After what took place at our first home football game two weeks ago??

Thankfully, after it was all said and done, this was an isolated threat that we identified between a student in our feeder middle school and one of our students. The middle school student was properly charged and would have no way of attending the football game. The student of ours receiving the threat wasn't going to the game either. Sadly, this latest drama took me completely out of this meeting, mentally and physically. I had to apologize and excuse myself to get back to school and iron out the details for how we would proceed with our plans for the game. Fortunately, not only did we have details of this threat, it was isolated between the two students and NOT broadcasted on social media …

The rest of the day remained busy with me immediately assuming my duties as a cashier during 4th period. After lunch, we tied up some loose ends to finish out the week. The football game was uneventful with us taking the safe route and providing more security than was necessary. Considering what took place at our first home ball game, we felt that the fans would appreciate seeing the officer presence … Apollo Eagles won taking several defensive stands throughout the game, 10 to 7.

Attendance for today was 89.58%.

September 13, 2021 – This weekend seemed pretty short— this effect takes place sometimes when we have a home football game on Friday night. It's already Monday?

Today started with a couple of messages from parents who had either called late Friday or early this morning. One was from a parent who wanted a copy of the curriculum used in his daughter's classes. This is well within the rights of parents to ask, so we started work in getting the curriculum together (starting with syllabi) and then going from there. Once the parent has looked over the syllabus for each course, we asked him to request any specific course curriculum that he wanted to research further. This parent admitted that he was curious based on the information about "critical race theory" that circulated on all the news stations over the summer. This hot topic made him curious as to just what curriculum our courses at Apollo HS followed …

The school nurse stopped by with a favor to ask. She wanted to see if I would call the parents of a student who had been a "contact" by another student who had tested positive for the virus. This particular parent was one of our "anti-mask" parents. I spoke with the step mother on the phone— it was a very cordial and calm conversation as I had described to the step mother the details for how long the quarantine period would last. This led to a phone conversation with the biological mother and the biological father, who were disappointed that I had contacted the stepmother (she was #3 on the contact list). The stepmother was married to the biological father. After complaining a little about how ridiculous this all is (mask wearing— the masks obviously don't work!) and the fact that the daughter has to be quarantined, I have come to realize in 20 years as a principal that some people just cannot be happy unless they are complaining about something ...

On the *personnel* side of this day, we found four classrooms in the upstairs of one of our sections with deliberate messes that were made. One had a red drink sprinkled all over the floor; one had a sticky substance spilled just inside the entrance; one had uncooked pinto beans (used for counting and measuring) spilled all over the floor; and one office space had chocolate syrup spilled. None of these rooms had any of these messes at the end of the day, Friday, when all of the teachers had left. We also had no events inside the building on Friday or over the weekend.

This "mystery" was quickly solved after reviewing camera footage and it was determined that one of the evening custodians was "retaliating" against one of the day custodians because they were "not doing their jobs" and leaving messes at the end of the day that should be cleaned up before they leave. This custodian is another individual who would not be happy unless he was complaining. In ALL my years of education, I have never seen something so *juvenile*. I will leave it at that ...

The rest of the day was "normal" as I spent my 90 minutes cashiering and taking care of loose items in the office at the end of the day. Most days, I take a walk around the construction area to see how the progress is going. We have had a major addition to our building that features two wings that will house the Engineering Academy and the Agriculture Academy. There are also several regular classrooms that will have mostly math, social studies, and some special education teachers. This addition was supposed to be complete mid-July based on the original timeline. As construction for education facilities goes, this has been delayed and we will likely not have full access to the new classrooms and offices until DECEMBER! ...

88.5% attendance ...

September 15, 2021 – Have I mentioned how much I LOATHE social media? I never have had the interest to engage from the earliest days of the social- media era for one simple reason: the negativity generated seems to me to far outweigh the positive. I may be an extremist, but I feel that social media may very well be the downfall of civilization. Some parents and anti-education people in general sit back and fill the platforms with negativity, false information, and conspiracy theories. Some of our most UNeducated members of society choose to educate themselves purely by what they read from social media. Do you want to be a BULLY? In 2021, it is SO easy. You don't have to push weaker kids around the playground and take a chance that someone may actually beat YOU up for it. All you need is a smartphone and any social- media account. There are a LOT of 10-foot tall people walking around these days, just because social media exists.

NONE of our students have lived before the time of the smartphone. Most of them knew how to manipulate their parents' smartphones at the age of two; some, **_better_** than their parents! Our students today cannot have conversations without them, cannot take their attention away from them for more than 10 minutes, AND, as a result, cannot look people in the eye and have a genuine conversation without feeling REALLY uncomfortable. Did I mention bullying? Oh, yes, ALL bullying in schools happens on a wide array of social media platforms, making it virtually **_impossible_** for administrators and teachers to see or trace. Yes, social media combined with the smartphone permanently attached to our students' hands may very well be the worst thing that has ever happened to education (BESIDES the Coronavirus Pandemic) …

Our students are currently caught up in a popular social media challenge going all over the nation basically encouraging them to steal items or vandalize school property and get it on video to share on the platform. ANYTHING in schools not bolted to the floor is pretty much fair game— students are taking the items and trying to hide them in book bags and videoing their "get away". The most accessible and unsupervised area that exists in schools is taking the hardest hit at Apollo HS— the restrooms. Towel dispensers, soap dispensers, faucet handles, hand sanitizer stations, and any other item that students can easily free from the wall. There have also been some teachers reporting that they have had some of their personal items taken from their classrooms. What is wrong with society when "challenges" like this become encouraged and celebrated among our youth (maybe even some adults!)? Thank you, social media!

Fortunately, SOME of our students are just bright enough to think that ONLY their friends will see this, think it is funny, and that NONE of the adults in the school building will have access to the video. UNfortunately, many of our students are smart enough that they know how to "dodge the authorities" and still be lauded as "heroes" in the eyes of the challenge crowd.

This is just one other obstacle that we have had to put resources and effort into than we really have to offer. The assistant principals and other personnel who have been "deputized" are spending time walking into restrooms (some even hanging out for a while), just to make their presence known and hanging onto hope that they may actually catch one of our unsuspecting students in the act. This effort has proven helpful, but not to the degree that we need that would have any chance of putting an end to the vandalism. We have too many restrooms to cover and simply not enough personnel to be everywhere at any given moment. Needless to say, we will be spending some time at our weekly Leadership Meeting to discuss what we can do to gain some form of control over this issue ...

———◆———

This day DID have a bright side. At some point midday, I was walking past one of our outer offices within the main office and noticed our front desk secretary in tears. She was barely able to control her emotions enough to tell me if she was OK. Through the tears and emotion, she explained that one of our parents had just dropped off flowers to her and thanked her for being so nice and professional to her when she stopped by last week.

On the day in reference, this parent had stopped by and mentioned that her father had just passed and she wanted to pick up her child. Our front desk secretary, being the person that she is, genuinely consoled this parent and went out of her way to let the parent know that we would be thinking of the family. This parent was obviously taken aback by the kindness shown by our front desk secretary and went so far as saying, "I am never treated this way when I stop by the 'other' high school." ...

After the parent left the office, the magnitude of all the trauma we have endured at Apollo HS this year swept through this office secretary and she just could not contain her emotion and tears. She removed herself and went back to the outer office, where I found her. There have been a LOT of hateful individuals confronting this secretary just because she was the one who answers the phone first. There are several hateful individuals who have no choice but to pick up their child because they have been quarantined based on contact-tracing and the virus. Again, they take their anger out on the person at the front desk. Through it all— the lockdown, the angst of the quarantines, etc.— this secretary and the other office personnel ALWAYS maintain the proper professionalism and poise in greeting our guests. The "lockdown sign-out parade" was, in all honesty, a spectacle to behold based on the kindness, smiles, and professionalism that this front desk secretary and her "crew" assembled at the moment displayed. I have told them all once, but it likely has not been enough.

After she described what had gotten to her emotions, I mentioned again how dedicated to her job she was and this is evidence of the impact that she is making on people. I encouraged her to keep up the good work! This is one of many times that I feel the urge to give a hug, but I withhold knowing that it is not the right thing to do. The best part of her response was her admitting that she had reached a point that she was ready to jump across the counter and choke the next person who was hateful to her ...

This HAS been a difficult year and the kindness returned by this parent was GOOD therapy— not just for the recipient (who TRULY deserved it), but also the rest of us in the office who heard the story.

September 16, 2021 – We had a fight today between two freshmen this morning between 1st and 2nd period. I had to be directly involved in taking down the information and determining "why" because our two assistant principals had a district meeting and our Dean of Students was absent. In times like this, it can be difficult being the ONLY administrator in the building— especially if multiple events are happening. Luckily, this fight was the only event I had to deal with before lunch and the return of our assistant principals.

As is typical, this fight started between the two students at the end of the previous day. One student was not where he was supposed to be (left the classroom at the wrong dismissal), and the two students had a verbal exchange caused by a misunderstanding of "playful behavior". That exchange at the end of the day led to the two students (once considered "friend ") texting each other back and forth that evening, calling each other names and making threats to beat the other one up. BOTH students felt 10-feet tall as they sat in the comfort of their own homes making threats to the other. The natural reaction would be to continue the threats face-to-face the next day.

This is a typical "fight" that takes place at Apollo HS. Most people may hear of a fight and picture the worst, but it is almost always between two individuals who were once considered friends who end up pushing or punching over what started out as a misunderstanding. The end result is 3- days suspension, assault charges filed, and 20 days of detention in another facility within the district before the students involved in the fight can return. Whatever the reason, the punishment and end result is NEVER worth the violence taking place to begin with ...

On a brighter side, I was approached by one of our teachers while I was cashiering at lunch who had AWESOME news to share. This teacher reported that she was scheduled for surgery to remove the stoma in her trach in December. This was a goal that she had set for herself and worked hard for after she had been told by her doctor that her health would likely not allow for the stoma to be removed from her trach. She had experienced a life-threatening event 18 months ago and had to work hard to get her health back in order so that this surgery could take place. With tears in her eyes and holding a finger over her trach to speak, she told me the good news ...

It is moments like these that absolutely MAKE MY DAY and keep me moving forward. When vandalism, fighting, and other events are bringing you down mentally as an administrator, it is the good stories that you receive like this that you hang on to. This teacher is a VERY special person to me and Apollo HS. I know I can speak for ALL of us in saying that we are proud of her for making this surgery happen ... AND we are so fortunate and thankful that she is still with us and working alongside us today! ...

———————— ◆ ————————

I very, very rarely miss school for personal reasons or for illness (I am BLESSED in that regard). In my 30+ years, I can count on my two hands the number of personal days I have taken and the same for the number of sick days. I decided earlier this week to take Friday off. A good friend of mine who I have not seen much since the beginning of the pandemic made me an offer that I could not refuse. Truth be told, I need a break with all that has happened since the start of this year ...

<u>September 20, 2021</u> – This weekend was a blessing and it helped me put some things into perspective. Friday turned out to be special from the beginning to the very end, as I spent some much-needed quality time with not one but two very close friends. These two are more like brothers to me than anything else, and we found a moment in our busy schedules that freed us up to connect in-person. We stepped away from the harsh reality that was surrounding us and we relished the moment. It was meant to be ...

Yesterday (Sunday), my wife Angela and I were able to travel to see our daughter play in her university's first public concert in 18 months due to the pandemic. On our way, we picked up our oldest two sons in Louisville to see the concert as well and had at least some driving time to spend with them. Although most of this day was spent on the road and in a rush to get back to our youngest son before bedtime, it was exhilarating to hear the power of a strong symphonic band play beautifully constructed music ... and our daughter was a small part of its creation. There were times I would close my eyes as the performance consumed me, sweeping me away from the reality that the world has to offer, and I was at peace. Man, what a moment ... What an opportunity to spend time with the ones you love ...

———— ◆ ————

Back to reality. There was NOTHING on this Monday that would come close to comparing to the last 72 hours. But then again, that's not how it works. It was good to get back to the work at hand with the positive experiences that I had in my mind and heart from the past three days. I was in a MUCH better place to move forward and roll up my sleeves.

In my absence Friday, I found that it was a semi-typical day with no major issues. Our attendance the last three days of this past week had finally risen above 90%. Still not where we want to be, BUT, slowly getting there.

Today wasn't much different. I spent my usual time at the cash register connecting with students and a moment or two in meetings trying to make for better experiences for our English Language (EL) learners. The vandalism in the restrooms and throughout the building is (we certainly HOPE) starting to decline. This may or may not be as a result of the letter I sent to all parents this past Thursday making the parents aware of the "challenge" and what our students are doing to take part. Whether the plea for their assistance had anything to do with this decline in the activity or not, it doesn't matter. As long as we have a chance to get back to the work that we were intended to do without the very irrational AND irresponsible activity we have had to distract us. Let's see if we can keep this more positive moment moving forward! ...

September 22, 2021 (Too many things _beyond our control_) – *THE* most frustrating part of my job as an administrator is to have an issue that desperately needs to be "fixed" and not being able to do the first thing about it. To start this year, topping the list as I have mentioned before, being short four custodians and at least three cafeteria staff gave us our biggest daily management challenge. I spent too many sleepless nights thinking about the unclean areas of our building, and I could not do anything about the fact that we did not have **_anyone_** applying for the $12+- per- hour jobs we had available. The cafeteria staff shortage? I did the only thing I could to help this obstacle and became a cafeteria lady myself. AT LEAST I had control over what I had myself do from 11:30 to 1:00 every day …

Construction … I have had very few GOOD experiences when it comes to construction and the educational setting. If ***commercial*** construction took as long as the construction associated with education (or, at least, the projects I have been a part of), Lowe's, Menards, Wal-Mart, and the like you see "'pop up'" in a community would GO OUT OF BUSINESS before they ever started! I have had very similar issues with the schedule and timeline on projects before as well as during the pandemic …

We have had construction going on at Apollo's campus since June of 2020 for an ADDITION of new offices and 25 classrooms. The original timeline had us moving into the new addition the second week of July. Although we could see the progress before our very eyes (or lack of), we ***believed*** what the construction foreman told us up until the first week in May: the building would be ready for us to move in. With this information, we ordered the furniture needed for this new addition and we arranged for the teachers who were moving into the new addition to box up their belongings before the end of the school year. I included the construction foreman in the email communication I sent out to the teachers about the procedures they needed to go through to "prepare for the move". Days later, the construction company declared that the new addition would NOT be ready before the start of school in August …

At the very next construction meeting, it was declared that they would have the "first floor ready by the end of August and the entire building ready by the middle of September". Piddle, piddle, over the summer with workers ending their day by 4:00. Piddle, piddle … By late summer, we found out that the building would not be ready before mid-October. We also became very worried that the "Connector" from the original building to the Gym area and classrooms would not be completed before the school year began and our students would be forced to walk outside to get from one location to the other. I almost forgot— the sidewalk to the gym was not poured, and this would cause our students to walk a quarter mile from the new student parking lot to the front of the school (instead of through the gym lobby). This prompted a "Come to Jesus meeting" with the construction company "brass", our superintendent, the architects, the DCPS Maintenance personnel, and myself.

It was July 21st and three weeks before the start of the school year. The Connector had walls but no ceiling or roof, and there was dirt between the student parking lot and the entrance to the gym lobby that they needed to enter our building. It was time for an "ultimatum". The contractors either had the Connector complete enough for us to occupy AND a sidewalk to the front of the gym lobby OR we had to delay the start of school ... and THAT was not happening ...

In 16 days, the sidewalk had been poured. In 20 days, the roof to the Connector, brick, windows, and doors had been completed AND sealed enough for us to occupy! This includes: A/C functioning, fire alarm and sprinkler system (otherwise, we could not occupy), and temporary lighting. It was a MIRACLE! In three weeks' time, it seemed like a legit construction zone and progress was being made! Paint on the walls came two weeks later. It is Sept. 22 and NOTHING has happened in the Connector since ...

Two weeks ago (Sept. 8), at the Construction Update Meeting, the foreman indicated that the timeline for **_project completion_** would be Nov. 18, with some aspects completed earlier. "OK," we thought ... This is **doable**. Construction completed by Nov. 18 would allow DCPS Maintenance and Technology to do their work in order for us to move in and be ready to start the 2nd semester (Jan. 4) in the new addition. At today's meeting (14 days later!), it was unveiled that the project completion would be Dec. 9 and would likely NOT leave us enough time to get the technology and "move in" complete before Jan. 4 …

@$&%#&^%#*^$!! At the time that I am typing this journal entry, NOBODY else at Apollo HS is aware of this. I don't care what excuse there may be regarding a shortage of manpower because of the pandemic and the luxury of free "handouts" since the beginning of 2020, THIS … IS … RIDICULOUS!!!

Oh, I almost forgot, we have **_another_** contractor who is due to start renovating the original areas of Apollo HS on January 4— this requiring us to relocate an entire section of our building and EMPTY the contents of that area in order for us to make this "renovation during the school year" happen. I STILL cannot believe this is happening. We have had more than our share of challenges to start this year at Apollo HS, and it looks as if we have several more headed our way …

September 24, 2021 – Yesterday was the last day for students this week because today is a Professional Development day for teachers. This is typically the day that we gather all of our assessment data from the previous year and disseminate the information to inform changes in curriculum, instruction, and planning for the purpose of stronger comprehension in our students. The only problem for this year is that we have NO reliable assessment data because of the train-wreck year we had this past year and especially the fact that not all of our students were required to take the state assessments. For 100% virtual students, the assessment was optional(?). For quarantined students, they did not have to take the exam either. WHAT was the purpose for us to even follow through with state assessment, KNOWING the data would be meaningless to us with NOTHING TO COMPARE to previous years? The STATE had it right in asking the federal government for a waiver ... the federal government held firm in their decisions and wasted money and everyone's time.

What we did receive that is actually helpful to us right now is the Safe Schools survey data that all 10th- and 11th- grade students who tested from last year responded to. These are the questions like "I feel my school is safe", "I have at least one adult who I can come to with problems", "My teachers respect my opinion", "Bullying is a problem at my school", etc. This is GOOD information, and we must consider that it is based on 80% or more of our current 11th- and 12th- graders ...

THIS is the data that we are going to wrap our Eagle wings and minds around today. Our Mission (developed Feb. 2020, just before the onset of the pandemic) is something that our adults in the building firmly believe in and stand behind. What is our STUDENTS' perception? This, along with our investment in tracking lost learning from the previous year, is what our "Dynamos " built our professional development day around. We conversed about important items to Apollo and for gaining back lost learning, we had an activity or two related to personalities and getting to know each other a little more, AND the Ag Department cooked out for us (burgers and dogs), all courtesy of an arrangement by our Culture/Climate Committee. THIS is how we roll at Apollo ... It was a GOOD DAY! ...

September 27, 2021 — One of the last things that I communicated on Friday to the faculty present for Professional Development (PD) was my thoughts on a new position that the district was offering in an effort to track down our most frequently absent students and work to provide resources they need to re-engage in school. These positions would assign individuals to three students that fit the description of "unsuccessful", and it would require the adults to spend three to four hours of their time (outside of the school day) to communicate, make home visits, and apply resources to reduce the barriers that are holding the students back. The intent for this program is definitely a good thing— if it helps five more students at Apollo HS be re-engaged in their learning, it is **_worth the effort_** without question ...

HOWEVER, most of the adults that I run into during the day are zapped. Many are putting in long hours to keep the plans and grades being entered in a timely manner. Some are not keeping these up as they should. I have witnessed too many of our "top" teachers struggling.

Based on this and my concern for the well-being of our staff, I posed four questions. Everyone was to close their eyes and simply raise their hand if their answer to any question I asked was "YES. "

- Do you feel overwhelmed at least once per week as a result of your work here at Apollo? 80% or better raised their hand ... Hands down, eyes closed ...

- Do you feel you are giving more of your personal time to get your work done than you should? 90% or better raised their hand ... Hands down, eyes closed ...

- Weekly, do you feel behind on your planning, grading, OR both? 80% or better raised their hand ... Hands down, eyes closed ...

- Are you already late on items that the administration has asked for like PGP, Self-Reflection, or any other task that has been requested? 20% raised their hand (this was a test to see that certain ones I knew were in this category would admit it!). Hands down, eyes still closed ...

My last statement summarized the activity: "If you answered YES to two or more of these questions, raise your hand". I could not see any hands down ... "OK, hands still raised, open your eyes!"

The teachers all witnessed that they were "all in the same boat". As I mentioned, if anyone didn't have their hand raised on the last statement, I didn't see them. I followed up by saying that I would not advise anyone who had their hand raised to be taking on any more. Their personal time and their sanity was more important! Also, the last thing we needed was for the teachers to be distracted any more with their teaching jobs! I certainly feel that everyone at the PD on Friday understood my point. While this program to re-engage some of our students to school and being successful was a GOOD THING, it really needed to be reserved for those who have the time to do their current job AND provide help to the students in the program ...

———•◆•———

I spoke individually with two "rock star" teachers today. My first was at the beginning of a teacher's planning period. This teacher, I have noticed this past week, was not his cheerful self, his head down in the halls as he was heading somewhere and looking very STRESSED. He is one who also had his hand raised for all four of my questions that I asked at the PD Day on Friday.

As I entered the room, I simply asked him if he was OK. I could tell the answer in his eyes. He admitted that he was battling. The new program that the Math Dept. had taken on was requiring more of his time. He admitted it was a good program and he wanted to learn more how to use it properly. Again, it was making his job as a teacher more challenging at the same time. He could not stand the fact that he was feeling 50% as a teacher, father (of four!), husband, and cross-country coach because he was so overwhelmed.

I asked him if there was anything that could be done to lighten his load. Cross-Country season is about 30 more days, but the problem is that Track doesn't start too much later (Indoor Track starts competition in the winter). He admitted to having all the right kind of help with his teams (other adult assistants), and he could not think of anything that would help him as a teacher. Taking a "day off in an effort to get caught up" usually ends up putting you further behind. He admitted the consideration that if something had to give, it would have to be coaching at some point. This individual LOVES his sport and especially his athletes. It would be a tragedy if it came to this …

I left this teacher with the promise that we were going to make it work and I did not want him to worry about certain items I had requested. We would find a way to manage and get to them when the time was right. I also asked him to reach out to me if he needed any assistance at any time. These are the meetings that I feel so helpless as a principal. Talking through what was going on MAY have helped this individual feel better, but I couldn't offer any solutions to ease his burdens.

My second meeting came after the school day had ended and most of the students had left the last bus. I saw a teacher struggling to carry a 5-gallon bucket full of laundry detergent while also carrying her personal and school items. I offered my assistance, for which she declined. I couldn't help but to demand that she let me. I had forgotten how heavy a FULL 5-gallon bucket is! …

On our way out to her vehicle, I simply asked how she was doing. I knew that she had been having trouble with a couple of her math lab classes (mostly behavior), but I had not heard from her directly. This teacher is one of our most veteran teachers and the current Department Chair. She has taught all levels of math and is VERY successful at bringing students to understand the expectations from Day 1 and consistently following up from that moment forward. This individual is an incredible teacher in that she knows how to hold students to her expectations while establishing a positive rapport with them. She is known to TEACH well and has plenty of time to get her daily plan achieved because she allows no "funny business" …

To my question, this teacher answered, "To be honest with you, Mr. Lasley, I am not doing very well." She described her struggles with at least two of her classes where she spends the bulk of her time calling students down and maintaining discipline. It is eight weeks into the school year and she has felt that she has taught the students very little. One class has a co-teacher, but both of them are bogged down trying to keep the students' attention and on-task. This 26-year veteran teacher was at her wits' end and leaving school IN TEARS. She was exasperated and embarrassed (she is NOT a "crier"), so I did my best to offer her a "divide- and- conquer" suggestion starting TOMORROW, if needed, and let her go ...

HOW COULD THIS BE?? Has the pandemic changed these students SO drastically that our "rock star" teachers could no longer manage them? These particular 9th- grade students missed out on the last quarter of their 7th- grade year when the pandemic started, missed most of their 8th- grade year (in-person at least), and now are starting their 9th- grade year like we have uncaged some wild animals. Once again, I feel the same helpless feeling that I felt earlier in the day talking to the other teacher. I couldn't offer much for this teacher to feel any better, but I realize at the same time that we HAVE TO do something or this veteran teacher is not going to last very long. The teacher is at her wits' end and the students are not learning. It is time for a change, REGARDLESS of what it might be ...

I realize these are **_just two examples_** (of the 84 teachers on staff), but these two have at least proved my point about not having the ability to take on any more. How many more are there? ...

September 29, 2021 – In the meantime ... School Report Card information went "live" today. Our district, like many others, is reeling a little bit because of the regression from the amount of lost learning from this past year-and-a-half. All districts agree and are quick to explain to the media that the academic data cannot be compared to previous years (not all students took the state assessment AND those who did were obviously ill-prepared after a majority of the year "learning from home"). One aspect that seemed to be most disturbing to the districts was the decline in Graduation Rate from 2020 to 2021. I am proud to say that Apollo HS's graduation rate INCREASED over this pandemic time period. It is not where we hope for it to be, but an increase is an increase. I would like to think that it was due to the extra efforts that our teachers put into getting our students to earn 360 half-credits over our Summer School on steroids June 2021!

Nevertheless, we have work to do, and we have been asked to see what we can do about our students from 2021 who did not graduate (9) and how we can work to ensure more of our current- year seniors are successful. Fortunately, the Leadership Team at Apollo HS is already on this! The problem is, we have several seniors who are already failing multiple classes, and a handful (4 or 5) who have not really "engaged" at all. Of those, there have been home visits and phone calls with no response. We have a couple of seniors who we feel may not even be in this area. The point is, we are ON IT. This is an "automatic" response that has happened at Apollo HS over the past few years— some of these efforts have been due to my influence and several were already in place. I inherited an incredible administrative team when I was hired at Apollo as principal, and I have been fortunate to have added a couple of "Dynamos" who only make this team stronger. More on the administrative team later on ...

I asked our Leadership Team to compile some "evidence" (List of 2021 NON-grads, list of current seniors and underclassmen struggling, etc.) for us to spend some time discussing at our weekly leadership meeting on Friday. In the meantime, we had our regular "work" to do. Cashiering at lunch, construction walk-throughs, etc., etc.

At lunch, "Darren" was wired up. He has made a point to come over to me as I am starting my routine before lunches begin and chit chat. On this day, he put his arm around my shoulders and asked me if I could send out another poll to find out how many students like the orange-flavored milk (gagging as I type), like I did for the sporks. The orange-flavored milk is a new item that is reported to taste like a Dream sicle. I am only taking the connoisseur's word for it. "Darren" apparently is one who LIKES it and is disappointed it was a "limited-edition release". I told "Darren" that I had been busy, but I promised to put something like that together and it would likely be after Fall Break … YES, Fall Break NEXT WEEK! As "Darren" goes back to his bistro table full of friends at lunch, he is cackling the entire lunch period for ALL to hear. I had to go back to him a time or two and remind him that EVERYONE can hear him. He is always polite, respectful, and does what he is asked. I can't help but to have a special place in my heart for "Darren" and the good handful of students I have made a direct connection with over the years …

Since Monday and my tearful conversation with two of Apollo's "rock star" teachers, my last item on each day's agenda is to pay a visit to one particular "rock star's" classroom.

On Tuesday, I had asked permission to join this teacher for class— she readily thanked me for that consideration. I spent nearly all of the class period in her room to help "monitor". The kids didn't act the way that they had previously and did everything they were asked by this teacher. There were times that it took a little effort, but they finally complied. This teacher has a loving heart and will talk to the students EACH in such a nurturing manner, but she is stern at the same time. It is all about BUSINESS, and these students are in this class because they have some skills and content that they have missed over this past year that they desperately need moving forward. If they cannot catch up, THEY will be on the list of NON-grads for 2025 graduating year. These students have important work to do, and I was there to ensure that there was NO "funny business". The students followed through and progress was made ...

Today, Wednesday, I went up a little later just to allow the class to get started. I experienced more of the same. One of our student aides is also assigned to help out in this classroom (20 students of HIGH need to one teacher can be very troublesome). She is a National Merit Semi-Finalist (the ONLY one in our district this year) and she is top-notch! She admitted to me outside of this classroom that she doesn't particularly enjoy this type of work (mainly because of the constant discipline that is required). If you remove the discipline distractions, she doesn't mind it at all. She also admitted that the classroom experience is so much better when I am in the classroom. I was happy to hear that from HER perspective. The BEST part of my efforts at the end of the day on Tuesday and Wednesday? I actually saw this "rock star" teacher smile again ... We are making the right progress!

October 1, 2021 (The Good, The Bad, and The Ugly) – The last task for me to complete on Thursday was to send an encouraging message as we entered Fall Break:

> Apollo Staff – I am sending this on the eve of our last day because I want to make sure this message gets out. Tomorrow will likely be busy!
>
> It is hard to believe that we are in October and even harder to believe that we have made it to Fall Break without having to use virtual days. I certainly hope that this trend will continue!
>
> Although we have made it to this point, I KNOW that it has

not been easy. ***I greatly appreciate everyone' s hard work and dedication to make this school year happen and I look forward to our work yet to come! ...***

Lastly, and most importantly, I truly hope that each one of you has the opportunity over the next 9 days to find your " Lake Cumberland" and give yourself a good recharge. Nothing major planned for me and my family, except ...

ENJOY! You certainly deserve it!

I try my hardest to consider the impact this pandemic has had on our staff, and I work to keep a pulse on the staff's well-being. As I have mentioned before, "finding your Lake Cumberland" is all about taking care of yourself and ensuring that your mind and body remains "in a good place". As of the time I am typing this journal entry, I have had one staff member respond to this email wishing me the same.

It's not that this email was sent with the intent for everyone to respond. I certainly would not have the time to sort through 156 emails and respond myself. The problem, for me, is knowing that this message IS being received and if it is having the impact that I am hoping for. I venture to say that a large number of our staff members aren't even reading them, but I would have no way of knowing for sure. Email has become an antique as far as communication goes. Very few parents respond to this form of communication and, unfortunately, it has been ignored by some "education supervisors" even when you reach out with a direct question or need. This, to me, is inexcusable no matter how ancient the form of communication may be.

———— ◆ ————

Yesterday, we had a fight break out before the school day began between two freshmen. The worst part about this fight isn't the fact that two of our students had friction between them, it was that an older student somehow knew that the students had exchanged words and he made a point to bring the two students together to make the fight happen! We call these students "promoters" or "Don Kings" whose sole purpose is to get to witness a good fight. Many times, these promoters will fill the opponent's heads with "I heard him call you a ___, " whether true or not, just to fan the flames until the smolder ignites into a full-fledged fire. Because these promoters are not typically the smartest of our students, this one chose a location that was in direct view of one of our cameras!

With the aid of the video and especially the actions of our "promoter", this fight was quickly sorted out with all three students getting sent home with charges being filed. The promoter didn't even make an effort to break the fight up— the fight just ended prior to adults getting to the scene.

When the promoter's parents arrived to pick him up, it didn't take long for us to see where this student got his personality. I heard commotion at the front office entrance, so I left my office to offer assistance. Both mom and dad were on the other side of the glass door, yelling and refusing to wear a mask. Our front office secretary was talking to them through the speaker system and explained that they would not be allowed into the office without putting their masks on. By the time I had arrived, nearly all of the admin team had arrived, along with our School Law Enforcement Officer (SLEO).

While he was talking to them through the door, they were shouting over him. "You bring my son here, RIGHT NOW!! You bring my son here, RIGHT NOW!!" "We don't care about the principal, we have already complained about him already!" Not that I haven' t heard these words before, but the odd thing is that I have never even had a conversation with this family. The crazed parents continued, "What is your name and badge number?" to our SLEO. He promptly shared what they had requested— not that it would help them much, because he was simply doing his job!

There were times that I felt that these parents were on the verge of being arrested, based on their actions. If they had tried to advance through the locked door, it would have happened. Thankfully, their son was sent up from the assistant principal's office within a couple minutes of their arrival. When this type of tense altercation is taking place, two minutes seems like an eternity. The worst part of the moment that we had was that a visiting parent was inside the office to witness and another student was sitting in the office waiting to be seen by our Dean of Students before I could get him to another location. It's bad enough when WE have to witness this type of irrational, uncivil behavior.

———— ◆ ————

Today, Friday, we have our weekly Leadership Team Meeting to start our day. We made an effort to focus on what could be done about the nine students who did not graduate in 2021. With little that could be done about these nine unsuccessful students, we started planning to focus on what we could do to make our current seniors successful by the end of this year. We also quickly determined that there were only two or three staff members at Apollo that we would recommend for the new district positions to help track down disengaged students. The bottom line was that the vast majority of our staff members are already overworked and overstressed with the working conditions that we are experiencing.

When I went back to my office, I received a note saying that the mother of the "promoter" from yesterday had called and wanted to speak with me. I knew without knowing what the purpose was for her to call that this was going to be a lose-lose conversation. One thing I learned early on in my admin experience was to NOT delay calls like this and to go ahead and grab that bull by the horns.

On the phone, this mother was very politely and calmly asking for an appeal and also asking to file a grievance against our SLEO. The mother claimed that her son was "the one who broke up the fight" and had no reason to be charged. She wanted the ability to see the video for herself. After I explained that she could not see the video because it contained confidentially protected footage of other students than just her son, I told her that her appeal would not be supported and that I had full confidence in our SLEO and his work. The mother asked if I had seen the video to be able to make that judgment. I told her that I hadn't and that I do not make a practice of following up on every incident that happens— others in the building have the authority to make those decisions without my influence.

It was at this point that I felt a shift in the demeanor of this mother developing. I asked her if this was the same person who was barking orders at the front office door just yesterday. I knew it was, but my point with this mother was that it didn't seem right that she would treat us the way she and her husband did on one day, then to make an effort the next day to "reason" through the situation and ask for any latitude. This was the spark that quickly rekindled the aggression that we'd witnessed the day before.

From that point forward, I could only get a couple of words in and the mother was cutting me off, yelling about getting a lawyer to be able to see the video. I explained to the mother that we WERE going to have a civil conversation OR we would have to end it. "I am being civil! We will just have to lawyer up and see you in court!!" This continued until I had to hang up the phone to end the conversation after telling the mother that we could no longer have this type of conversation.

Mother continued trying to contact the Guidance Office and "appeal" to the grade- level counselor responsible for her son. She also called the front office to speak to someone else. Neither attempt proved to provide her with what she wanted. All of this attention on her son made us realize how unsuccessful he had been the past couple of years and how he had very little chance at graduating with his peers. Because of this last discipline issue and the charges filed, this prompted us to make the call to see if we could get him enrolled in the district's alternate secondary school setting. There is a good chance that he will be enrolled there to start after Fall Break ...

What an exhausting week! I am VERY ready to take a break! Normally, I would work a couple of days over Fall Break to get some things caught up and to also check in with our 261- day custodians to see what they are working on. For my own well-being, I am going to limit my appearance at school to ONE partial day. Although these types of interactions with parents are very few and far between, the negative confrontations can take a toll on an administrator's psyche. I am going to fully take advantage of the Fall Break experience and try to focus more on the number of GOOD, RATIONAL, and HIGHLY SUPPORTIVE parents who send their children to Apollo HS …

October 11, 2021 (The Day After Fall Break!) – The DAY after Fall Break, it is always tough to get back into our routines— and I am just talking about us adults! Fall Break was a refreshing week for me as I used my time to close out some special projects that I had started at home. I am an avid woodworker and thoroughly enjoy creating projects of my own design in my mind and constructing them in my small woodshop at home. I am at peace when I am working on these projects. For most people, doing your own home renovation of the family room, from floor to tongue-n-groove wood ceiling, would cause them stress. For me, it's GOOD THERAPY …

I was ready to come back to school based on the work that I was able to get done, finalizing a few things in our family room renovation. It was also good for me to see other adults in the first part of the day and see similar smiles on their faces that I had to be showing on mine (all through the masks that we wore!). It was good to hear their stories for how the break was for them.

This morning started out positive, not just based on the stories I heard from different adults and my own mood, but also when I found out that our Cafeteria Team was FULLY STAFFED with 16 ladies for the first time in over 18 months! This was TREMENDOUS NEWS based on what we had gone through the first 8 weeks of our school year. I was informed that I would no longer be needed as a cashier at lunch, unless someone couldn't make it and a substitute couldn't be secured. I told our cafeteria manager that I would happily stay "on call" and that we would make that decision day-to-day. WOW— for the first time in 8 weeks, I would have my 11:30 to 1:00 back and be able to do my

" usual" work as a principal. Although this is a VERY GOOD THING, there was a part of me that already missed the daily connections that I made with students. I know these students are in good hands and (hopefully) I would be needed to come back and help out from time to time ...

This good news led to hearing other good news, like the EL student that we found a way to get help with his GED. This student should have graduated at this point, and we were able to convince him that his GED would allow him the opportunities he was looking for. It is just the beginning of this process and will likely take the rest of the year, but we have him motivated and moving in the right direction for the time being!

I spent a good portion of the rest of my morning working on trying to get more help for the students that we had lost since the beginning of the year academically and due to chronic absenteeism (or both!). This issue for Apollo HS was enough for us to handle pre-pandemic, and it has grown significantly these past two years. We MUST continue to work at this issue and think outside the box— the normal resources that we have to support this growing concern wasn't enough before the pandemic began and it certainly isn't enough now.

My midday routine that I normally spent as cashier I spent in the lunchroom helping the other administrators monitor. When I had the chance, I would stop by "my" old cashier stand and ask the cashier-in-training if she needed any help. There are two lines that meet near the same point, so there is another cashier nearby who can cover for you if it is ever needed. Because you sit so close to another individual, it gives you opportunities to talk with them during down times. I jokingly explain to the cashier-in-training that it takes YEARS of training before they let you "graduate" as a full-fledged cashier. Both the veteran and the "newbie" appreciated the humor that I had offered ...

My afternoon consisted of getting the shipment of tables and stools put together (with the assistance of our day/evening custodial staff) for our NEW Senior Eating Area in the new Connector to the new addition. Another GOOD thing to witness at the start of this day after Fall Break was to see the Connector now 85% complete with the walls all painted, the windows in and sealed, and the drop ceiling in place. The only thing left is the tile floor that would go in at the very last with all of the floors in the New Addition. Still, this was a drastic change from what we had been using in the Connector with temporary lighting and no ceiling. This area is very brightly lit up and it has the brand- new appeal that makes you feel good to walk through it. I am looking forward to introducing this new Senior Dining Area for our students on ENL tomorrow morning ...

--------◆--------

I have to say that 90% of my day on the first day back from Fall Break was a very positive and uplifting day! This is hard to pull off on any day after a long break. The worst part of my day was having a conversation with **_another_** (the third in the last eight school days) "rock star" teacher who was tired of the struggles she was experiencing in a class of advanced students. The issue has evolved since the beginning of the year, but the underlying culprit has been the negativity shared by a handful of parents on social media that has spiraled in other directions for this teacher in question. Her frustrations were painfully evident and I did the best I could to give her support, knowing that she was going into a conference with one of her parents and our instructional coach the very next day. The words I chose in this meeting with her, I'm afraid did not hit the target I had intended. But I let her know that I supported the direction she would choose for this student and the entire class. I hope it will be enough— I hope that her meeting tomorrow is a win-win for her, this student, and for her class moving forward ...

October 13, 2021 – There are times that you have to just drop what you are doing and take care of what is most important— being 100% true to your values. As a principal, you have to be prepared for those adults who will confront you with a situation that involves family so that they cannot be at school to perform their duties for a day or sometimes a handful of days. There are times, in an emergency or death of a loved one, that you have no notice for getting the staff member's classes or obligations covered. IT DOESN'T MATTER! ... Without batting an eye, you must relay to this staff member that they "have more important things to take care of than work". Even if it means YOU are the teacher for the students in that particular classroom, the staff member MUST be relieved so that they can attend to what is most important ... There is NOTHING more important than family ...

Today was MY turn to focus on values in taking care of family needs. My wife, Angela, and I have been **_blessed_** with four children. We are VERY proud of each of our children and what they have each accomplished; our three oldest (Todd, Troy, and Lauren) are each charting their own paths and currently contributing to society in their own special way. There is nothing that makes parents more proud than to see their own children being **_productive_** members of society! Yes, WE are PROUD of our kids!

Our youngest, Aaron, just turned 16 this past Sunday and is a very special young man in his own right. Aaron was born deaf and struggled entering this world due to a virus that complicated Angela's delivery. It wasn't long after he was born that we found out the extent of his profound hearing loss. We made the decision to provide Aaron with the gift of hearing and made the necessary arrangements for him to receive a Cochlear Implant just before his first birthday (at the time, one of the youngest patients to have the surgery). We hated to do this to the young man, but we just **_knew_** the benefits would far outweigh the procedure ... (?)

That is … until we discovered that Aaron was autistic. Not only was Aaron autistic, he was far enough on the nonverbal end of the spectrum that we soon discovered that the sensory issues he would have would prevent him from keeping his cochlear implant in the "operating position" on his head so that he could effectively hear. Unless we were near Aaron, we would not know where he had taken off the device and where he might have discarded it …

This was a disappointing as well as challenging setback for Angela and me, to say the least. We made the hard decision not to "fight" the issue of keeping Aaron's cochlear implant active on his head (whether he liked it or not!) and made the decision to continue loving Aaron for the very unique and challenging young man that he was.

Just after the start of the pandemic, Aaron had his first seizure. Thankfully, I was at my shop when I saw him on his "playground" start seizing and I witnessed most of what happened. This is one aspect of being an educator that you absolutely must prepare yourself for— at some point, you WILL have a student that is prone to seizures. We educators, thankfully, are trained what to do, what to look for, and to KEEP TIME.

Since that first seizure in April 2020, Aaron has had two more and has been officially diagnosed with a mild form of epilepsy. He is on medication for this and, so far, has not had any seizures since his last one in July of this year. It would take some tests to determine what is causing Aaron's seizures and what would be the best medicines to support him …

Today, we had a sedated EEG (brain scan) scheduled for him at Norton's Children's Hospital in Louisville. Up early, nothing to eat or drink, 90-minute drive, nervous as a cat on a hot tin roof, waiting, waiting, waiting, finally the procedure (longest 75 minutes of my life!), and back on the road and home at 4:30 pm. We were just happy to be able to make it through— Aaron, of course, but ALSO Angela and I. Hopefully, this procedure will provide the results that we need to give us (and the doctors) the answers needed to better provide for Aaron's health and safety. That is all we can ask and expect ...

———— • ————

Although I told my Leadership Team that I would be out all day and the reason why, I let them know I would be "on call" for anything that was needed (checking email and text). This was pointless, as we ALL know how little reception you get in the middle of a hospital. The team KNEW better than to fall for that and nobody made an attempt to contact me for anything (other than prayers and well-wishes). That is one of the best things about being a part of an exceptional Leadership Team. I inherited a strong admin team when I was hired as principal at Apollo HS, and I have helped develop an even stronger leadership team that we have today. Whether I am completely separated from the action like today OR tending to my "duties" for 1.5 hours in the middle of the school day, I KNOW that everything is being taken care of ... regardless of how difficult the challenge may be. Again, NOTHING is more important than family ... and, my Leadership Team fully understands that! I will find out tomorrow if today went smoothly or just how much of a train wreck it might have been ...

October 15, 2021 (End of 1st 9 weeks) – Yesterday, I was needed to work as a cashier at lunch because of a shortage within the kitchen. This was good for me for getting the opportunity to connect with the students again. I am hoping that I will be needed once per week or so, and I feel certain that it may become more frequent. We shall see ...

It is hard to believe that we have reached the midpoint of the first semester. The 2nd 9 weeks always go by faster because of the holidays and the activities/events that take place at school. I am hoping that the trend of fewer positive Covid cases and the increase in attendance rate continues. If this happens, let's hope that there is a noticeable positive difference in our students' grades mid year. As of now? ... Failure rates for our students are through the roof, despite our teachers' best efforts to reteach and re-engage them. Something must change ...

There is an obvious trend of concerns that have been written up to this point in these journal entries. The sum of these concerns, plus a few more, include: the morale of our teachers; those teachers "defeated" by their work; increased student behavior issues; lack of candidates available for classified positions; attendance rates and "lost" students; failure rates; AND the overall concern that there will be a noticeable increase in the number of teachers retiring at the end of this year. We administrators have a LOT on our plates under what used to be "normal" conditions. The challenge to find solutions to the aforementioned concerns is palpable and enough to break the spirit of the best and brightest leaders. This reminds me of the analogy I once heard from one of my grad school professors: Sometimes, in administration, we are served an "elephant" to eat. The best way to eat an elephant, you may ask? One bite at a time ...

Enough with the negative. The "Made My Day" moment that I was gifted today was the student who approached me at some point around lunchtime as if we had known each other for a long time. My traditional greeting for running into students is, "How are you doing today?" This greeting prompted the very cheerful response, "Today is an AWESOME day, Mr. Lasley. I am finally getting adopted!" With the biggest smile I could manage behind my mask, I congratulated this student and told him how happy I was for him. I do not know this student's name and I cannot recall if I had ever seen him before. He is one of a good handful of students who are "lost in the crowd" when you have 1,400+

students in a school. Regardless of this fact, I was HAPPY to hear this and look forward to keeping up with this student in the future …

October 20, 2021 (3rd Day of 2nd 9 Weeks) – I had made the decision to start off pointing out the positive for the 2nd 9 weeks and try not to continue a trend of gloom. Monday began in true Monday fashion with a cluster of little things that went wrong enough to mess up our day. Nothing individually catastrophic, but combined to challenge our work. So, I passed on writing about Monday. The BEST part of Monday was being asked to cashier again through lunch. I readily obliged and enjoyed the interactions with the students …

The best part of Tuesday was the recognition of our School Law Enforcement Officer for his daily dedication and service to the safety needs of our staff and students, but especially his swift actions that kept all of us safe during the Aug. 26 Lockdown and the violence that took place the next night at the football game. Because we cannot have assemblies with all 1,400+ students in the gym (because of safe-distancing), we decided to have the recognition in the Commons Area before the school day began. The perfect timing was just before the bell rings for all students to head to their 1st period classes, when the capacity of the Commons Area was at its peak.

The staff all knew this was coming, even though our SLEO did not, and most of them had made their way to the Commons Area to witness and cheer him on for his dedication to OUR safety. The superintendent, the Director of Pupil Personnel, and Channel 25 News (Evansville) were all present to witness the presentation as well. The message I gave was clear— we cannot take such dedication for granted and we need to show our appreciation for the swift actions that were taken at these events to keep us all safe. Based on the reaction of our staff and our students, I would say that they agreed that this was long overdue …

———— ♦ ————

TODAY, Wednesday, was a GOOD DAY from beginning to end! This week is Spirit Week due to us playing our rival school in the district on Friday in football. "**_Detest_**" may be a harsh word for some in reference to how they feel about their rival, but it is likely true for most others. For Spirit Week today, students were allowed to dress up in character for Halloween, and it always creates a little more energy than usual. I will lay you odds that our attendance is at a high point just because of this allowance! Even though there is an overabundance of "energy" that is experienced on days like this, it appears to have produced a more positive than negative vibe overall.

After ENL, I was visited by a junior football player who had brought his "posse" with him. Monday, he had approached me with the consideration of having, at least, a modified Pep Rally with Juniors and Seniors, or even Seniors Only. Since the very beginning of this school year, we adults (ESPECIALLY students) have longed for the opportunity to have the "normal" events that our students have missed out on the entire past year. Up to this moment, we have never even considered having a dance or Pep Rally because of the distancing restrictions we are still under.

However, positive Covid cases have reached a lull AND our district has adopted the "Test to Stay" program that allows anyone who is determined a contact for a Covid-positive individual to be able to test **_negative_** and still remain in school (instead of 10 days quarantined). We have been organizing a 300-person- limit Sadie Hawkins Dance because of this "game-changer" program for Friday night after the game … OUTSIDE on the Soccer Field next to our new Football Stadium. Thankfully, the weather is looking good for us to have a Staff Tailgate event, Football Game against our District Rival, AND a Dance all rolled up into one evening. Why not a Pep Rally before the end of the school day?

I told this young man that I liked the way he was thinking, but I would need to give it some thought, get approval to do so from the District, and speak with the Admin Team about logistics before I could make a decision. He returned with his "posse" yesterday, but I was on a mission in another area of campus and could not see them. Someone in the front office jokingly told them that "he will not see you unless you have your student ID". Nine students with IDs were walking into my office this morning to see what could be done about the Pep Rally as well as a personal "ask" for the dance …

By the time the students were walking into my office, we (the Admin Team, Spirit Club Sponsors with District approval) had already worked out details for what we were going to do with the revised Junior/ Senior Pep Rally. As I have mentioned before, THIS is the best part of my job! These students were respectful, and they listened intently as rational citizens as to what we were allowed and what we could not be allowed based on the conditions established by the District and local Health Department. We talked about what had been laid out as far as the Pep Rally was concerned: juniors and seniors only, live-streamed for the 9th/10th- graders, and 15 minutes at the end of the day. We discussed what we could do to get more interest in the dance, but they understood by the time they left my office why we couldn't allow students from outside Apollo HS. It was a good meeting. Before they left, I asked if I could get a picture of them showing their IDs ... Awesome setup for this day ...

I quickly moved to an observation of a tremendous young teacher during 2nd period. She plans extraordinarily well, connects well with students, has a firm command of the Spanish language, and uses a variety of resources to enhance the learning experience for her students. Every student followed through with what she asked, and there is evidence of mutual respect ANY time I visit her classroom. For this 30-minute observation, I can't help the feeling of wanting to be in her class and join them— I do not understand much of the Spanish language, but can connect some based on what I know about French. With the issues that we are having in other classrooms reconnecting our students to learning in general and how to "play" school, this observation took me back to pre-pandemic times. What an incredibly awesome experience! I could not leave this teacher with ANY growth items to consider or any other feedback than very positive. This was one of a number of "Made My Day" moments on this Wednesday. How refreshing!

I had a few more positive connections on this day, but the last one I had capped off and summed up the day that I had. As I was walking into the office after the post-conference I had with the tremendous teacher I observed, I saw my friend "Darren" waiting at the front entrance with all his classmates and his teachers. He was wearing a witch's hat and cloak for his Spirit Day costume. He sees me and asks, "What about my Orange-flavored Milk poll that you were going to send out?" I reminded "Darren" that I said it had been a busy week and that I promised to have it out by the end of the week. "Friday?" "Yes, Darren— by Friday." I couldn't help but to turn the questions in his direction: "Why didn't you dress up today, Darren?" He tells me "I DID!" and mentions the character that he dressed up as. My response? "Oh, sorry, I couldn't tell any difference ..." This was a GOOD day, indeed ...

October 22, 2021 – Yesterday, the grades for the 1st 9-week grading period were made final. Reports were being made today by the Guidance Department for the number of failures that have been recorded. There is no question we are seeing an unprecedented number of students failing classes, compared to any other 1st 9-week grading period. The troubling statistic is the number of students who are failing four or five or ALL their classes. These students are just not engaging in their work (multiple 0's) and, typically, multiple absences. We have our work cut out for us.

I asked the Leadership Team at our weekly meeting to prepare to divide up our lists of failures and meet with students as well as contact parents. We also need to see if any teacher contacts have been recorded in Infinite Campus. If this is not the case, the teachers need to initiate the contacts. My worry is that the leadership team is going to be overwhelmed with the failure lists and the contacts that will need to be made, even after the contacts made by teachers.

I had an early meeting off-campus with area principals, superintendents, Directors of Pupil Personnel, and the Department of Juvenile Justice as well as the District Attorney. The topic of this meeting was to discuss the concern for the increase in violence and extreme behavior in our schools. Fighting has increased and the number of weapons charges (off-campus and not school related) has increased as well. Yet, these juveniles who have been charged are still enrolled in a local school. The mutual concern from the group was that it seems like only a matter of time that the violence finds its way into our schools. Another mutual agreement among the stakeholders at this meeting was that we ALL owned this problem and that we must come together to find solutions.

During the course of this meeting, I took the group back to Aug. 26 when Apollo had the unfortunate lockdown when a look-alike .40-caliber BB gun pistol was brought onto campus. I explained that this incident is as close as anyone wants to come to an actual event. Even still, I described how the event "scared the hell out of everyone" and how it has taken weeks for our attendance to climb out of the cellar. 86% the week of the lockdown led to an average of 88% two weeks later to slowly become 90%, and finally and consistently staying above 92– 93%. For an event that prompted 0 violence and 0 injuries, it has certainly taken its toll on the Apollo community.

I also took a moment to explain that the difficulty every one of us sitting around the table may be experiencing at the moment will only ***increase dramatically*** in the near future when the number of certified teachers in our classrooms decreases. To explain my point, I have had more conversations with "rock star" teachers this year, "picking them up" due to the conditions, and especially the unexplained behavior in many of our students (mostly freshmen!). These teachers have each given me the indication that they will likely retire at the first moment they are able. This is the worst thing you want to hear from our "rock star" teachers!

Although I had to leave before the meeting was over, I feel it was a good start and that everyone realized the topics are critical enough that we must communicate and be more consistent in expectations of charges being filed. At the least, I feel that the districts will be made more aware of students being enrolled in our schools who have had previous charges. At least this way, we will have 24 hours to make a decision for how these students should best be placed, while keeping the rest of our student body and staff safe.

———— • ————

This Friday DID have its positive moments. I had the pleasure of being asked if I could help cashier at lunch. This provided some student connections that I needed. Regardless of what may be going on or any issues that may exist, this duty I have assumed most of this year always finds a way to ground me and help me put things into perspective.

I also had an abbreviated formal observation of a "rock star" teacher who elected to go ahead with the observation, even though it would be cut a little short because of the Pep Rally. Although I felt that this might not be a good idea because of the obvious distraction that this class of juniors would have because of the Pep Rally at the end of the day, I was quickly put in my place by how much of a command this teacher had for her classroom instruction and especially the respect the students had for her and her expectations. They completed a weekly quiz, moved on to some note-taking in the transition from the Roaring Twenties to the Thirties and the Great Depression, and finished up by assigning some work they need to at least start (could finish Monday) ...ALL before the Pep Rally and not so much as a "peep". I was simply AMAZED! ...

The Pep Rally was the icing on the cake for this day and an incredible way to cap off the week. Although we only had juniors and seniors in the gym (underclassmen had the event live-streamed in their classrooms), there was enough energy to FEEL the presence of the entire student body. What a joy for us ADULTS to see and hear! This was the first Pep Rally that Apollo has had in about two years. The students came through on the challenge I had given for them to bring on the positive energy and to show their school spirit. For a 15-minute event, this Pep Rally was one of the more powerful experiences that I and the other adults who witnessed it have had in a LONG time. I can only hope and assume that the students felt the same way …

October 26, 2021 – Once per month, we have a District Principals Meeting with the district department leaders, the Asst. Superintendents, and the Superintendent. These meetings always happen in conjunction with the monthly Board Meeting. We principals are always kept "in the know" with changes to Board Policy, lingering issues that are related to the district, School Law and Legislation changes, and there is typically a Professional Learning experience that is added that we can share when we return back to our schools. Under "normal" conditions, this information is very helpful and typically appreciated, although I cannot say that I have always been 100% attentive based on things I had going on back at school …

Today, I can say that I felt relieved that there is much more of a focus on the current concerns that we are dealing with in schools as we continue to battle through this pandemic. We have been asked to make a concerted effort to share our gratitude for the work of others, including the "forgotten" bus drivers who are the first and last to see our students on any given school day. Not just this critical group of individuals, but the other people in our buildings who make our daily work possible. For most schools, I would say this naturally occurs (maybe **not to the degree** that we should), but it is comforting to know that the district leadership are fully aware of what we are facing.

The unanimous decision is that we need to check in on our NEW school employees to make sure that they each have the resources and support they need, and we need to check in with them again before the end of the semester. I have asked the Apollo Leadership Team to take this one step further and check in on ALL of our employees (classified as well as certified) and make sure they not only have what they need, but that each one of them is in a "good place". With eight Leadership Team members, this can be accomplished, and I feel that we will have covered 90% of our 156 employees by the end of this week. Each leader is checking in on the professional aspect of their jobs as well as also asking how everything is going at home— trying to make a connection and effort to reinforce that we care about their personal well-being equally as much as we care for their professional work at school. For me, these conversations have been powerful, and I _**feel**_ that the same can be said about the rest of the leadership team, but I can't always be sure ...

I came back to the school with a good feeling for what the district was focusing on. I had to quickly transition back to immediate school needs, and because of the timing, I missed out on the call for me to help cashier at lunch. It wasn't a dire necessity, as it turned out, but they could have used some help. Instead, I had to stay in my office to prepare for the faculty meeting we planned for tomorrow (Wednesday), and I needed time to organize the failure data. One of the "dynamos" was preparing the information for our teachers to let them know that State Assessment was back on the table; 100% expectation with 0's given for any student who did not participate (unless they had a _**state-approved**_ medical exemption).

I spent the end of the day in one of our intern teacher's classroom for a formal observation. Very sad to say that I have not spent any time in this teacher's classroom prior to today, even in an informal walk-through setting. I at least know the instructional coach has. The unfortunate truth is that I have not had the time, based on the other work I have had and the other immediate concerns that I have had to address.

Either way, being in the classroom (unless the lesson is a total train wreck!) is where I enjoy being the most. Again, it is about being a connection to not only the students, but to the educational experience that will prepare them for their future that I was made to be a part of. For this intern teacher, her classroom is far from a train wreck. In fact there is evidence she has established a positive learning environment and mutual respect between her and the students. While it may be a little rough around the edges, there is no more concern for her than with any intern teacher I have seen. I finished my day as I left her classroom by writing up my observation notes and made last preparations for what I needed to start the following day …

October, 27, 2021 – This day was a blur from beginning to end, but it had more than its share of drama and unwanted excitement. Three fights occurred today— ALL involving the freshmen class, who act more like 7th- graders (or caged wild animals).

Before the day even started in the breakfast line, one male student pulled down the pants of another male student. The obvious embarrassment initiated "game on" and, yes, assault charges being filed. Thankfully, the victim of this "Ha-ha" moment kept his underwear in place during the attack. Still, the damage was already done …

Before the second fight occurred, I had the opportunity to check in with one of our teachers who had lost their father to a very unforeseen stroke the week before. I also had the opportunity to make up for not being able to help the lunch ladies by cashiering during lunch. The troubling feeling that I have midday is that our two assistant principals and dean of students were all attending a district training that started just before lunch. These are the individuals who are instrumental in managing our students and any misbehaviors during lunch. Although our SLEO and our paid lunch monitor are also present, it is our administrators who do all the "heavy lifting".

Thankfully, the lunch periods all went by without any major mishaps. I had the opportunity to observe one of our veteran teachers in the afternoon, but that is when all the "fun" that the rest of the day had in store for me started.

I was 10 minutes into my observation (and thoroughly enjoying the experience) when the teacher's phone rang. Because I was near the phone, I answered, only to be disappointed that the call was for me. My secretary informed me that I was needed in the office due to none of the other administrators being available to address the fact that three young ladies were found in one of our Auxiliary Gym restrooms and a "cloud of smoke" was visible when they exited. I informed my secretary that I needed someone to process this questioning of the three young ladies (along with the SLEO) and that I did not want to interrupt my observation for something that was not an emergency.

Upon completing my observation time just a little bit early, I went to the office to take over the interrogation of the young ladies and the searching of their book bags for any device or cause to create "smoke". As I was finishing up with the last young lady, I heard individuals in the outer office very excitedly calling for me to let me know that the second fight for the day was taking place in a certain area of the building. As I started making my way in that direction, I ran into an adult and a student who had informed me that the fight had been broken up and that the individuals involved were headed to the office.

It didn't take me very long in this investigation to determine that this fight happened for no good reason at all. The aggressor assaulted the victim, essentially, because the victim had "aggravated" him. Upon watching the video with the SLEO, it was a full-on assault where the aggressor was waiting outside the boys' restroom with one of our "rock star" teachers standing nearby. This teacher takes her entire class to the restroom to avoid having the twenty interruptions in a forty-five minute classroom period. The aggressor launched into the victim when this teacher (and other students in class) are only 6 feet away!

As the school day quickly came to a close, I made sure to contact the grandparents of the aggressor to inform them as to what had happened and that their grandson would be charged for assault as well as disciplined to the fullest extent that the school district would allow. Not that it mattered, but the victim never had an opportunity to throw a punch or do anything more than to try to protect himself.

The regular school day ended and my concerns were with the "rock star" teacher who had witnessed the assault, on HER time. What was more troubling than this unfortunate aggressive experience was that this "rock star" teacher was one that I have had several conversations with this year and have had to "pick up" off the ground a time or two. I have visited her classroom with the very class of students who witnessed the assault, because of the class's lack of discipline and attention for the work we needed to instill in them to be successful enough to earn a credit in the foundational class. To see her at the end of the day as we were preparing for the faculty meeting, in tears, saying, "I just can't do this any more", was the gut-blow that nearly brought me to my knees ...

Then, there was the third fight that occurred between a student from another school (not in our district) and one of our students waiting to board the bus to go home. Apollo is a transition-point for some students who have to change buses in order to get on the right one to get them home. This non-district student picked a horrible day at Apollo HS to pick a fight ...

October 29, 2021 – It's been a long and exhausting week, based on the events that have taken place. In need of a positive "pick-me-up", I decided to finally follow through with the setting up of the Orange-Milk Poll that my friend "Darren" has been bugging me about. I had promised him I would have it ready by last Friday and I let myself get too engaged with everything else I was involved in to follow through on my promise. I decided not to let "Darren" down and I took the five minutes to prepare the Google Form and had my secretary send the link out to all students. On ENL, I mentioned the Poll and for students to look for the email ...

Our weekly Leadership Meeting took place and we worked to wrap our minds around the increase in fighting and extreme behavior in our freshmen, our concern for increased failure rates/lack of engagement in students, and other items we deemed equally as important. What a tough position to be in, when you consider the other concerns that we have in keeping the teachers and staff in a "good place" mentally and physically and the fact that we cannot find enough candidates to fill cafeteria and custodial positions.

We decided that the failure rates would be best communicated in a formal letter explaining the three, four, five, or all six classes that the students were failing. Any parent who receives this letter will be requested to contact the school for a conference with one of the administrators. Teachers would communicate with the parents of students who were failing their class ONLY or students who were failing their class and one more. Hopefully, by making all these contacts, a good number of our students would step up and do what it takes to be more successful by the end of this semester at Christmas. Time will tell.

I have a feeling that two or more of the most recent cafeteria staff are no longer working with us, for some reason. As principal, I wouldn't know this due to the cafeteria hires all being interviewed and processed through the Food Service Manager for the district. Either way, I am finding that I am being asked at least three times per week to help cashier at lunch, and most of these days I see that our Athletic Director is doing the same. Because today is the last day of the week before Halloween, all the lunch ladies dressed up as **crayons**— each representing a different color. They all had crayon t-shirts made to finish out their uniform, and I found the gray crayon shirt in my chair they had gotten for me. What an HONOR to be considered one of the group! I put on my crayon shirt and wore it with pride ...

Just after lunch, the District Office of Teaching and Learning team stopped by to go on a Learning Walk with me as we visited five classrooms. I had set up for us to see a couple of veterans, a co-teaching classroom, a novice teacher, and one of my choosing. Since we recently had been informed that state assessment is "back on" for this year with no exemptions or exceptions (unless medically approved), I decided to focus on two math and three English classes for our visit. Two of the classrooms we visited were of one novice and one veteran English 10 teacher. My reasoning for choosing these was two fold: 10th- graders are assessed in reading at the end of the year, AND I wanted to show evidence that our teachers were collaborating in their PLC's (Professional Learning Communities) to provide consistency in our teaching of "like courses". This is especially important in core classes.

Because we are all on "edge" with everything else going on, I made sure to inform the teachers that these visits were happening by sending an email just prior to lunch. These teachers did a wonderful job and had everything that they are expected to do in an observable format for the visitors, and the students were actively engaged in what they were asked to work on. This is nothing less than what I expected for us to see, as these teachers bring their 'A' game as much as humanly possible and have the same routines and expectations, regardless if visitors are expected or not.

The best part of the visit that I had no way of knowing would happen: the last teacher we visited was the veteran English 10 teacher who had fourteen students absent out of thirty on her roster! While we were in the room and observing the students working silently on their web-supported grammar program, I asked the teacher if this was typical. She said that she has been fighting this level of absenteeism from time to time. One day most are all present and another day 10 or more would be out. The frustrating part about it was the work that it created for her in trying to get the students caught up with their work. I emphasized what she was saying by nodding my head in understanding and told her to "hang in there" as the OTL team and I left her room.

Once back in my office to debrief on our classroom visits, the OTL team complimented the teachers and the way the building looked (clean and organized). I made the point about our concerns for absenteeism and the fact that our teachers cannot do their jobs effectively when students are not in their classrooms. Point made and received …

Before I left for the day, I was informed of our official attendance for the day: 88.98%. Abysmal, considering the ground that we had made to improve over the past couple of weeks. We are in desperate need of some help and solutions for our continued attendance woes! …

November 2, 2021 – The first Tuesday after the first Monday in November is Election Day, except when there are no elections to be held. I had the misfortune of speaking with a group of teachers just after Fall Break about the next break being Election Day. I did this out of habit, more than anything. When we realized my mistake, we made it a "good laugh" moment where the teachers acted so dejected and overly emotional for not getting the day off. At the time, I told them I would make it up to them and get donuts if they would stay and not walk out in protest. Although we shared another laugh, I made the decision to follow through. Yesterday, I announced that there would be twelve dozen donuts by 7:30 am in the Teachers' Eating Area. As you would expect, it was a hit ...

On ENL, I revealed the results of "Darren's" quick Orange Milk Poll. Of 260 participants, 70% had not tried it (think the concept sounds disgusting?), 22% disliked, and 8% LIKED Orange Milk. Sorry, "Darren"! I mentioned for others to be sure to try the new version of milk and I would keep the poll open for them to make an informed decision. The funny thing is that this poll had no real purpose other than to satisfy my good friend "Darren", and it has taken on quite a bit of talk around school! Before I made it back to the office, one student stopped me in the hall to let me know they had just asked their 1st period teacher permission to go try the Orange Milk. This student wanted to report to me that it was actually good!

Back in the office, we had back-to-back ATIP Cycle 1 meetings with the four "Math Pros" (District Math Specialist, Instructional Coach, Mentor Teacher, and myself) supporting the two intern math teachers. Each intern had a very promising start to the year, and each one provided strengths that would carry them far into education. Both needed small tweaks to adjust their teaching or their questioning, and we also followed up by establishing peer observation opportunities for both to engage in. Being that third-party observer to experience another adult teaching topics that you teach in your own classroom gives you a better perspective with ideas and strategies to take back to your arsenal. Both interns seemed so receptive to our feedback and left our positive meetings prepared to work on the growth items we had offered them ...

I found out late that I was needed to help cashier during lunch again, so I made plans to be there to help by the start of the 2nd shift. Because this has almost become a daily need again, I told the cafeteria manager that I would begin assuming that I was needed each day. If this was not the case, she could just let me know. As usual, the lunch connections that I made with the students and some of the staff that come through the line gave me the lift I needed on a busy day.

As I finish up my last student going through the last shift, I always go ahead and get back to the office to "get back to work" and see if I missed any calls or visitors. It wasn't long after I entered the office that a fight broke out between two females right in front of the Guidance Office. Yes, another freshman fight! As with a majority of the fights among this class of students, there was little reason to justify the extreme behavior of hitting another person in the face. All that one of the girls could come up with to answer the simple question, "Why?" ... "She was 'mean-mugging' me." This is an expression simply meaning "getting a stare- down". I simply cannot get over WHY our freshmen class is exhibiting such extreme behavior. Based on what we have heard from other schools, we are not alone ...

Knowing that one of our veteran teachers was out today for a doctor's appointment and the challenge of her 6th period class, I decided to visit her classroom to help her substitute get the class started. With the difficulties that our "rock star" teachers are having with some of these classes, the subs stand a decent chance of getting steam rolled. As luck would have it (very unfortunate for the students who need consistency for learning), I found that only seven students remained in class (due to absences) for this sub teacher. I stayed just long enough to leave an impression with my presence and left to come back to the office to start closing out for the day.

My secretary reported to me that 142 letters to parents of failing students were prepared and ready to be sent home this afternoon. These letters are being sent based on students failing three, four, five, or ALL of their classes. The letter lists the classes with a current failing grade, and it explains that "your son/daughter is in danger of an alternate education setting for next school year and potentially not graduating with their classmates". Each letter finishes by asking the parent(s) to call the school to set up a conference with an administrator. Once these letters are mailed and reach the hands of these parents/guardians (sometimes grandparents!), I wonder how many of the 142 will actually follow through with contacting the school. I venture to say that a vast majority will not and that we will have to make the effort to track the parents down, potentially making a home visit to make that contact ...

Having had enough for one day, I packed up and headed for home ...

November 4, 2021 – On ENL this morning, I decided it was time to offer everyone some advice. With all of the negativity that exists in the world, I encouraged all of our students to be a part of the GOOD. Too many times, people do not say "thank you" when someone opens a door or when they are given something. I mentioned that I do my best to greet all staff and students that I see every morning and throughout the day and how good it makes me feel when a student greets me first. I also mentioned how disappointing it is when you greet someone and they do not reciprocate the greeting. I encouraged everyone to do something GOOD for someone today— hold a door open, help someone in need, greet people you see regardless if you know them, and, if nothing else, SMILE! ...

As I returned to the office, I looked at the schedule I had on my calendar. We had another ATIP Cycle I meeting with a teacher that wasn't a true intern, but needed some guidance due to being away from education for a number of years to raise her children. I have a lot of respect for people who are true to their values and make these decisions. For this teacher, she just needed some help reconnecting to current standards and teaching strategies.

I also had a formal observation with one of our novice teachers whose intern year was the year the pandemic started. This teacher has been doing tremendous work and has also stepped up to co-sponsor a couple of clubs this year. My concern when I see this is someone taking on too much. I have taken the time prior to her accepting sponsorships as well as times like now to revisit that conversation. There have been times this year that I could tell that she has been delayed in responding to communication, or "distracted", but I have not seen any indication that it was getting in the way of her teaching. In education, we ALWAYS need teachers who are willing to sponsor. However, it is never worth developing bad habits in what is promising to be a tremendous teacher. For now, no major concerns, but it is worth coming back to the conversation from time to time.

Back in my office, I had just a few minutes to wolf down my sandwich I brought for lunch before I needed to report to the cafeteria and my cashier station. I often laugh (to myself) when teachers or anyone else complains that they do not have enough time to eat lunch. Thankfully, since going to a full 30 minutes for lunch, this complaint has been stifled. I completely understand how hard it is to release your class to lunch, get your lunch, and find a space to eat and be ready to receive your students back in your classroom 30 minutes later. I have been there before! The irony is that there are so many times that lunch for me has been taking 5 to 10 minutes to eat a sandwich at my desk while I am still working on something or standing inside the Commons Area monitoring students while eating a salad or something I have grabbed from the line. Yes, I could MAKE the time available for myself. It is just not worth the trouble it creates on most days ...

At "my" cashier stand, I was pleased to start hearing what I thought were more thank-yous and greetings from my students. One student went so far as saying, "I heard you on ENL this morning— are you having a good day today?" I also heard more students reciprocate greetings in the halls throughout the day as well. I certainly hope that this continues! The fact that there was another fight today during lunch (NOT freshmen) did not detract me from feeling good about the positivity exchange I was hearing. It's amazing how small efforts sometimes make the BIGGEST impact! ...

After all lunch shifts had ended, I decided to grab a hard hat and walk into the new building while construction was going on to see how it is coming together and how much progress has been made since they have enclosed all entrances with plastic. The last day I was in the building was October 12— the first day of school after Fall Break. To be honest, from what I saw today, I was hoping to see more complete. Only 35 calendar days are remaining between what it looks like today and December 9 (the day that the foreman indicated would be "final completion day" at the last construction meeting I attended). With the Thanksgiving holidays coming up and weekends to decrease the number of actual work days available between now and Dec. 9th, I left the new building NOT feeling very hopeful ...

On my way back to the office to close out this day, I reflected on how busy this week has been— what a whirlwind! I left campus with hopes that tomorrow will be a POSITIVE and UPLIFTING day to finish off the week. An overall uplifting school day spilling over to an exciting home playoff football game and a victory for the Eagles would be the positive energy I (we **_all_**) need to complete this busy week ...

November 10, 2021 (Special Addition – _PARENTS_) — I have held off on adding any entries in this journal this week because it has become "the usual", and I wanted to avoid sounding too repetitive. Not to minimize any given day "in the trenches" in education; each day brings its own highs and lows with **_something_** positive to hang on to. Instead, there is a trend that has developed over the course of the past two weeks that I feel the need to focus on ... PARENTS.

First and foremost, EVERY school has parents who support what the adults in the school are trying to achieve on any given day. Apollo has more than its fair share of parents who appreciate what we are doing, and there are times they will let us know about it. The problem is that in the past two years we have heard more from our disgruntled and, at times, irrational parents than we ever had before the pandemic began.

In the past two weeks, I have heard from one parent who e-mailed a lengthy explanation for why we should reconsider punishing her daughter for not having her Student ID and to consider ways of re-minding her to bring it to lunch every day. Her daughter was electing not to eat lunch to avoid receiving a DM (Discipline Mark), and her daughter should be reminded by her teachers to take her ID with her to lunch. Before this mother ended her lengthy email, she finished by threatening the Civil Liberties Union and taking her "case" to the school board and beyond if she had to in order to advocate for her daughter. This email communication was this mother's **_first attempt_** at communicating her concerns for the DM(s) her daughter received by not having her ID.

Another mother this past week at least CALLED to voice her con-cerns; her daughter had been served scalding hot mashed potatoes and it had burned the roof of her mouth. This mother wanted something done about it. Her daughter is a senior at Apollo. I PROMISE, I am not making this up!

First, I am not sure mashed potatoes have EVER been served "scalding hot" in our cafeteria. Second, and even if that **_was actually_** a possibility, should **WE** be held responsible for 18 year-olds who have had a momentary lapse of reason and forgot HOW to eat without burning the roof of their mouth??

I am forever thankful that these conversations are resolved without reaching my desk. KUDOS to my secretaries who have "talked through" these conversations and, at least, made the parent think that "something was going to be done about it". Of ALL the issues that we have to be concerned about at Apollo HS, "scalding hot mashed potatoes" would not even make the Top 100. As Charlie Brown would say … GOOD GRIEF! …

Too many of our parents today use social media as their source of information— the adult "pool party" where all kinds of misinformation is shared freely, only to get everyone attending worked up over issues that aren't really **issues**.

Too many of our parents base ALL of their information on what their child is telling them. At what point in the history of mankind did parents take what their child has told them as 100% factual? I'm not saying that we call all of our children "liars" and to not believe ANYTHING they say. I'm talking about statements like, "my teacher is mean to me" or "my teacher isn't teaching and we have to teach ourselves", taken as "Gospel" based on their children's complaint.

Too many of our parents (yes, I'm saying it) are prepared to "charge the Capital" at the drop of a hat. They have become anti-authority and are teaching their children not to trust authority and not be ashamed of letting anyone know how they feel about rules and expectations. A perfect demonstration of this is the young lady (9th grader) who interrupted me in the middle of an explanation I was giving one of the assistant principals for the "wrong" she had done in the classroom, proceeded to give her full rendition, and **_then_** gave me "permission" to carry on with what I was saying! ...

Whatever happened to the days of the FIRST step (out of respect and courtesy) being a phone call to school to speak with an administrator about concerns (OTHER than scalding hot mashed potatoes)? Even better? A **_scheduled_** visit to school without "demands" or without threats to your job or of litigation.

TODAY, I had the pleasure of having one of those meetings with the parents AND the child in question that was long overdue. This concern most likely originated from a "social- media feeding frenzy", but then again, maybe it didn't. Either way, the parents had not connected successfully in having a phone conversation with the teacher, and the parents and teacher had not successfully connected by having a face-to-face parent/teacher conference (likely through no fault of either). Yet, as of November 10, there had been nothing more than email conversation and the student not completely sharing the "whole truth" for what was going on in the classroom.

I arranged a meeting today at 4:00 pm to take place, after our faculty meeting, with both parents, the teacher, our instructional coach, and myself. To say that we educators were a little nervous as to how the meeting would go was an understatement. I promised both the teacher and our IC that I would keep the meeting to 30 minutes to respect **_THEIR_** time with families and to cut the meeting shorter if it took a less than positive direction. Here we go ...

After introductions and the apologies for our delay in meeting, I allowed the parents to voice their concern. Their son has NEVER struggled in math and he was making good grades in ALL his other classes. I made sure to explain (and take the blame off the teacher sitting in front of me ... ROCK STAR, I might add) that the past couple of years has taken its toll on the loss of learning in our students, especially in math, AND our advanced students have seen their share as well. I went on to say that I have observed in many classes the loss of confidence in our highest achievers.

This went back and forth with the teacher giving her rendition for the struggles the student was having on assessments and what she was seeing and not seeing during class. Mother broke down a little bit at one point, but the entire conversation was 100% civil and respectful. In the end, it came down to 3 pieces of advice that I (we) gave the young student to be successful moving forward:

1. Advocate for yourself and ask the teacher questions before, during, or after class.

2. SHOW YOUR WORK on tests and quizzes, especially when the instructions say SHOW YOUR WORK. In math, this is an absolute necessity for "us" teachers to know where the mistakes are made. "We" teachers can help you more by seeing your work!

3. Attend ESS (Extended School Services) offered 3 afternoons and 3 mornings each week.

Bottom Line— IF students follow these three pieces of advice, they will be more successful in the end. If a student follows these suggestions without fail? The rest is ON US! …

The meeting was held for just under thirty-five minutes, and the parents (and student) left with the indication that they knew we wanted the student to be successful AND we were willing to do our part (and more) to see that success was the end result. More? I even offered my assistance to the student to stop by if nobody was available to help before or after school to work on some problems (this is something I enjoy almost as much as cashiering at lunch!).

This meeting was actually an uplifting part of my day. _**I cannot stress enough to educators and parents in this day and time the POWER and authenticity of the face-to-face meeting over ANY form of communication**_.

November 12, 2021 (My Friday AM routine) – Every Friday morning, without fail except during Lent, I have a routine that I particularly enjoy around 7:30 am. I go through the breakfast line and get biscuits with gravy and two sausage patties. There is a particular cafeteria lady who ALWAYS serves me, and she goes out of her way to find the most perfect biscuits and perfect sausage patties to put on my plate. She goes so far as to reach into the warmer behind her if she cannot find the biscuits or sausage to her liking! She then pours on the gravy with the large ladle as we exchange our "Happy Friday!" or "Have a Great Day!" greetings and I head to the Staff Eating Area adjacent to the Commons Area to enjoy ...

I grew up on a dairy farm from the time I was in kindergarten until the time I graduated college. It was hard work, in the simplest of descriptions, but there were SO MANY pleasures living on the dairy farm provided me that I took for granted and I miss dearly to this very day.

My mamaw was always in her kitchen, on the original homestead, as she was responsible for cooking large breakfasts (served AFTER morning chores and milking was complete), large lunches, and large dinners for several individuals each day (my father had five siblings). We ate big for each meal but we did plenty during the day to work off every calorie. I loved eating at Mamaw and Papaw's, and breakfast was always my favorite time— not just for the food, but the company that came with it!

Every Friday morning at school while I hover over the breakfast plate I was graciously served, I can close my eyes and be taken back to the farm and eating breakfast at Mamaw's table. It has been going on forty years since my grandparents moved out of the original homestead and into their last home before passing away, and I can **see** the back entrance to the back porch/boot room, I can **_hear_** the slam of the screen door behind me as I walk past the cellar, and I can **smell** the breakfast that Mamaw is carefully and lovingly preparing for those she is about to serve. On the plus-side of fifty years old, I can forget some of the simplest things that happened yesterday, but this memory that I come back to **_every Friday morning_** is one that is emblazoned in my mind and will never be forgotten. For that moment, I am at peace and I am happy! ...

———————•◆•———————

I had a drop-in but formal observation today with a phenomenal teacher from bell to bell. The reason for the unexpected drop-in on a formal observation is because this individual is overwhelmed and cannot find the time to enter grades in a timely manner or even respond to administrator emails. If our evaluation process was based solely on "Maintaining Accurate Records" and "Professionalism", this person would be removed as a teacher at the end of the day ... Turn in your keys! But, then again, there are FAR more important details that a teacher has to be responsible for, and THAT is what makes this teacher special ...

As I walked into this teacher's classroom, I noticed a slight "surprise" and a mention of "no worries about a dog-n-pony show today" as the teacher chuckled and smiled. Just to be clear, there is NOTHING "dog-n-pony" about this teacher ...

From the moment I entered the classroom, I was mesmerized and amazed. This is another one of our very troubled and uneducated

Algebra I classrooms where our students are struggling. This teacher was in the process of teaching the substitution method for solving systems of equations, and he had the students eating out of his hand. This teacher has a knack for explaining concepts and teaching skills by putting everything in a "language" that the students can understand. Here is an example:

A student asked how the teacher substituted and came up with the equation that they had written on the board. This teacher paused for a moment and asked the student, "Do you like Buffalo Wild Wings?" Yes, of course! "What if you made your order that came with chips and you did not like their chips? Can you replace the chips with more wings?" NO! "What about a filet mignon steak?" NO! "Why can't you?" Because they are not the "same"! "Ahh! But we **could** replace chips with fries, couldn't we?" YES! "That's what we are doing when we use the substitution method and use $x = 5y+3$. x is your chips and $5y + 3$ represents your fries ... " This teacher wove the "usual" tapestry that I witness every time I enter their classroom. I leave mesmerized and secretly wishing I was back in school and in their classroom. BRILLIANT!

———◆———

The last connection and conversation that I had today was with the teacher who had communicated earlier this semester about the surgery to remove the stoma from her trachea that she was hoping for in December. I ran into this teacher after the day had ended and the last remaining students were trickling out of the building. She informed me that she had her confirmation visit with Vanderbilt yesterday and heard from her doctors that the surgery was a "Go"! This teacher had successfully lost over 100 pounds after a life-threatening event and had reduced her blood-sugar levels to the point that her stoma removal was VERY possible. This was music to my ears! Of all the good that might have been experienced on this day, THIS sealed it for me. I told this teacher how happy and proud I was for them for their hard work and dedication to make this moment and especially the surgery a possibility. Despite all the troubling things that happened this week at school, all the positives that I experienced consumed me. Life is good! We will make time for the "troubling things" starting Monday AM …

November 16, 2021 – Tuesday was a challenge. I am being criticized by superiors for continuing my work as cashier during lunch and that I am neglecting part of my job as principal during that time. That may be a harsher way of interpreting the message delivered, but that's how it was received. The most disappointing aspect of that communication was the insinuation that I am working as a cashier when it is not necessary and that there ARE actually other alternatives. Does it mean anything that our Athletic Director has also been working as a cashier because of the shortage in the kitchen? Fifteen teachers were out of the building and an adult short in the main office where my secretary had to split time at the front desk and the attendance office. We have no room to give! …

The best part of my Tuesday was in the EL Newcomer classroom observing our EL Newcomer Teacher. The Newcomer class is made up of English Language Learners from another country who have entered school at Apollo for the first time in the United States. Many of these students speak very little English, and of all the students in this classroom there are at least six foreign languages spoken among them. Needless to say, this is a tremendous challenge for the one teacher plus a temporary aide that we have in the room!

The students are a pleasure to be around. They are cheerful and they want to belong, despite their struggles understanding everything that the teachers (and principal) are saying. Today, these students are learning the value of coins/bills and how to properly count money. This is an obvious skill that will be very important to them moving forward in our country. Although the "Money" song that was shown on a video about the values and names of all American coins was NOT as appreciated as the teacher had hoped, a few of the students tried to sing along. And, yes, the song came with a "catchy" tune that I couldn't help repeating in my mind throughout the day. The students **_did_** enjoy counting the fake coins and money that they were given by the teacher and working in groups to ensure each student had someone to guide them.

Although native languages are spoken among the students while they are working in groups, the adults use 100% English as they reinforce the proper vocabulary surrounding money and making change. The students slowly pick up the language a few words at a time, and they are happy to have the opportunity and, again, be a part of Apollo HS!

The rest of the day went downhill from that uplifting classroom experience as we had two fights that occurred, one happening just behind my cashier stand as I had turned to disinfect my hands to get ready for the next lunch group. I was the first one to arrive at this fight scene, but the two students had already fully "engaged" and the damage was done. Once again, our challenge to lessen the amount of extreme behavior in our students INCREASES as we have now experienced more fights already this year than all of the years I have been at Apollo **_combined!_** The absence of human contact for long periods of time by our students being virtual this past year is coming back to haunt us. This is the only explanation that I have. The absence of human interaction coupled with the extreme behavior that has been demonstrated all over the media this past year (January 6, 2021, riots in several cities across the nation, etc.) has taken its toll! In some respects, it feels as if we are dealing with feral children ...

I made a pitch to our Asst. Superintendent for Student Services that we have to try **_something_** different. Our "backlog" of students going to the CAI (Center for Alternate Instruction) will only continue to grow. The fact that we have students in fights today (or with drugs) and that they have to wait for an intake meeting at CAI until Dec. 14 is not acceptable. The Asst. Superintendent did not disagree and he promised to speak with the Superintendent to look into other options.

My "ask" as we ended our conversation was that we consider making a student virtual for the rest of the year if they reach a certain point in discipline. For students with drugs, or assault, or too many extreme behaviors, they continue their education but be in the "comfort" of their own homes and out of harm's way for the rest of our student population (and staff!). If we don't consider these alternatives, the by-product of all this misbehavior will be losing teachers at the end of this year. Again, no disagreements coming from the other side of the phone.

The last thing I find out before I leave for the day? We have 4 unfilled evening custodial positions out of 8 for tonight. Our personnel shortage woes strike again! ...

November 17, 2021 – There are times as a leader that you come to the realization that you are wrong. Despite your intentions and any good will that you feel you have accomplished, you are still wrong. Admitting to others that you are wrong and you are sorry for your mistake is the greatest challenge as a leader to overcome ...

I blew my stack" today. I have reached a point that the stress I am experiencing is not healthy (professionally as much as personally) and I am taking things far too personal. What I have established as my way of helping the cafeteria ladies out on a (now) daily and permanent basis is wrong. Although I would continue finding a way to help these ladies, especially in a pinch, I have to realize that the teachers need my support in the same way and I must find "balance".

I "blew my stack" with one of my immediate supervisors over an email that I took far too personal in regards to finding other alternatives for the cafeteria shortage. Before our follow-up meeting was over, we both apologized for our part in the misunderstanding and we agreed to "move on tomorrow". As an afterthought and reflection on my way home, I responded to my supervisor's last email communication with another apology:

> *Again, I'm sorry … Although we may have our different views on how we need to get our work done, we are still on the same team. This job has become far too difficult not to keep this in mind. You are correct that the staff AND teachers need my support equally and I need to find a way to achieve balance. I have already made plans to do just that moving forward …*
>
> *I hope you understand - will see you tomorrow …*

On the positive side, we established a milestone and some good connections today at Apollo. More on that for later this week …

November 19, 2021 — This has been a mentally exhausting week. Yesterday, the Department Heads and Leadership Team (about eighteen adults) worked three hours after the school day ended to score Apollo HS against the accreditation standards for AdvancED. I have been a part of this process at least three other times and I cannot remember the written standards being so complex. We all agreed that the standards may as well have been written in Greek. Before the night ended, I had a headache— and I am not one to get headaches! The best part of the experience was the small catered meal that we all shared together, and that ***we all worked together*** on the three categories of standards, no matter how difficult to understand they were!

Earlier in the day yesterday and because of the rash of continued vandalism that we have experienced in our restrooms off and on again, continued fighting and extreme behavior in our 9th graders, AND several students with multiple F's, I decided that it was time for our Leadership Team to have a discussion. Here is the email that I sent out to prepare them for our weekly Leadership Team Meeting:

> *Apollo Leadership - Considering the challenging times that we are in, I would like for us to prepare for a conversation tomorrow with your personal thoughts on the challenges that deserve the most attention. I suspect that there will be several thoughts and not a collective concern, but this is a good starting point. Please be prepared to bring answers to these statements from your **own** perspective (do not speak with anyone else on the team):*
>
> * *Apollo's biggest challenge that needs to be addressed now is _____*
> * *Possible solutions for addressing the challenge are _____*
>
> *Thanks for your work!*

This morning at our meeting, we started off with this topic right away. The team members each shared their responses to my request. The Leadership Team's answers were no real surprise to me-- Concern for the number of students out of class, the level of teaching in some areas of the building to keep our student's attention, the societal lack of trust/respect for authority that is spilling over into school, the misbehavior in our students and the fact that we have multiple students failing multiple (or all) classes. The Leadership Team left no stone unturned!

As we further discussed, we came to a consistent theme that we determined was a critical issue that we needed addressed— that teachers become the adults in the classroom and learn how to tell the students, "NO!". We determined that there was no good reason to allow students to go to the restroom during a forty-eight minute class period, and some of our teachers are going to the extreme of allowing students to go to the restroom as soon as the class period begins! Some of the team even mentioned an example of teachers who allow students to go to the restroom after they have returned to class from a 30-minute lunch(?). This was certainly something that we would need to change and give some direction on ... and SOON.

One of the items that came up in discussion that was the hardest to stomach was the comment that teachers were not being held accountable. It may not have been a sole judgment intended for me, as principal, but, then again, maybe it was. This statement came from one of the "dynamos" that I have mentioned before. What made this worse is that I feel that the other dynamo was in agreement (at the very least, **_didn't disagree_**).

This day was busy and I had a full agenda that did not include having time to stop by any classrooms. For each item that I worked on and every place that I ended up in our building, I couldn't get the topics of our meeting out of my mind. Regardless of how it made me feel, I knew in my mind that we HAD to grab the reins and address what is going on to **_regain_** control. The conditions that we are working in are hard enough (disengaged students, low attendance rates, lingering pandemic), the OTHER issues are ones that WE should be able to control. "We" being EVERY adult in the school. As this week ends, I have come to the conclusion that it is squarely up to **_me_**, as principal, to initiate the action that will make this challenge go away. The very first step I must take is to communicate my thoughts with my two assistant principals and get them on board, OR hear from them any thoughts of a plan that might be better. Then? ... Communicate to the faculty and staff what we must do to correct this situation. When? ... MONDAY (or Sunday afternoon). Although this is a 2-day week leading into the Thanksgiving Holiday, this issue needs our immediate attention and cannot wait any longer ...

It's 9:10 pm on a Friday night, and I feel so relieved to have typed this entry in my journal. I can now have some peace this weekend ...

November 23, 2021 (Thanksgiving Edition) – With the help of the advice from my assistant principals, we determined that we needed to use these two days heading into the Thanksgiving holiday for communication purposes in getting our teachers on board with the new expectations, making sure the students were aware and giving them two school days to adjust their routines AND, most importantly, informing our parents. We need a couple of school days to help talk some of our parents through our reasoning behind not allowing students to use the restroom during a forty-eight minute class and what opportunities our students have throughout the day to make pit stops.

As these two days have unfolded, I am thankful that I listened first to my assistant principals to "pump the brakes" on initiating the new expectations right away. Having the time to think this through and talk to a **_couple_** of irate parents (one who was making the threat to "get us all fired") allowed us the opportunity to realize that we had some time that we could alter our bell schedule to allow one more minute in our passing time between classes, with hopes it might help with any extended lines that might form in our restrooms in some areas of the building. By and large, the vast majority of our rational students and parents **seem** to accept our reasoning for enforcing this restroom expectation, and they **seem** to appreciate the adjustments we are making to help out. Come Monday, we will see how enforcing this expectation goes. For now, it sure **_seems_** that I have the staff's support to make this work.

———◆———

Reflecting back over these past thirty years or so, I have been blessed to have been afforded the opportunities I have been given and to be where I am today. I thank God for these opportunities as often as I can. I thank God for the people I have had the fortune to work with over the years, because it did not take me long in education to realize that there is a part of every individual you have worked closely with in your career that you carry with you every single day you move forward. There is no such thing as a "self-made" man or woman in education. Anyone who thinks that this may be true for them is sadly mistaken ...

I would like to pay homage to the individuals who hired me for my first teaching and coaching opportunity at St. Romuald Interparochial School and those I worked closely with that year. I will never forget the teaching experiences I had that year and also winning that first basketball game of the season for a team that had gone winless the year before. It was my St. Romuald experience where I met my wife, Angela, as I taught and coached her younger siblings. Yes, as they say, the rest is history ...

I must show respect and pay gratitude to the individuals I taught with at Cloverport Independent Schools as we taught together for twelve years in the trenches under five principals. It was there that I was given my opportunities for leadership as a young Athletic Director and also a taste of administration my last year (while still teaching). I met, quite possibly, the best teacher and individual that I have worked with in my 32 years of education. I still admire to this day his approach to education and his connection with people in general. I had not only his tutelage but one other I leaned on as my unofficial mentors who helped guide me and reflect on what to continue to do and what to consider doing differently that helped keep me on a straight and narrow path. Many of our "reflections" and "private lessons" occurred on evenings on weekends as we enjoyed a beverage through the haze of cigar smoke. One of my fondest memories that I will always remember is the two-night trip that my mentors and I spent canoeing down the Nolin River to the Nolin Lake Lodge from the bridge in White Mills, Kentucky. My mentors trusted me in the planning and navigating of this trip (without the aid of cell phones and Mapquest!) and we made it through to the end, beaten up and exhausted! Although we spent much more time canoeing across parts of Nolin Lake because of a miscalculation of mine, the trip was spiritual in a lot of ways and it solidified the bond that we all had with each other.

I spent 13 years as an administrator at Hancock County High School; 2 years as an Assistant Principal before being hired as the Principal. It was Hancock County that I learned the most out of leading people and how to rally around a shared purpose. During this time, we managed the highest marks in the region in College and Career Readiness while recording the highest ACT average in HCHS history. The Class of 2012 will **_always be_** the smartest, most competitive, most genuine and respectful group of students I have ever had! I worked with some tremendous educators at HCHS, many of whom I still run into on occasion today. I have developed at least one friendship from my time at Hancock Co. that still grows to this day as we reach out to each other and help with professional as well as personal obstacles that challenge us. I am forever grateful for my time at Hancock Co. and the education that Hancock Co. Schools provided our children.

Little did I know that I had so much more to learn after leaving Hancock County Schools! The experience I had as an administrator certainly made all the difference as I took over as principal at Apollo HS exactly one week prior to the first day of school in August 2016. It also helped me develop a better plan for leading others by affording me the opportunity to learn from any mistakes I had made in my prior experiences. This current year is like none I have seen in 32 years, as the experiences I have written about in this journal have vividly described. I have a lot of respect for the individuals I have worked closely with at Apollo High School and continue to work with today. I am blessed to have the most talented leadership team that I have mostly inherited upon hire, but I at least hope that I have had part in the initiation of some and the development of others that remain on this team. We have been through a lot just in these past two years, and the dedication of these individuals and their commitment to the success of our students is something I will never forget ...

Yes, Rick Lasley is a BLESSED man! *Happy Thanksgiving to ALL those individuals* I carry with me and who have helped develop me into the leader and educator I am today ...

November 30, 2021 – Thanksgiving Break 2021 was a much needed time for me to "unplug" and recharge. I took full advantage of the Wednesday through Sunday experience and spent time with our kids, removing myself completely from work. I typically do not do this and will bring a little work home or spend at least half of Wednesday working at school. NOT this year— the time I spent away was priceless and couldn't have been spent more wisely ...

Reality sets in on Monday AM when you try to get up on your "normal" work clock and you feel you haven't slept at all. It was good to see everyone saunter into the building, students and staff, most likely feeling a little "off" just as much as me. The best part of this Monday was the fact that our district had made the decision to change our MS and HS Covid Protocol to a "mask optional" understanding, and somewhere around 80% of our adults and students took full advantage of it.

I'm not taking sides, but it certainly was refreshing to see FACES again! This was the first time in over eighteen months that we have NOT been required to wear masks inside the building.

But, that was YESTERDAY ... Today we initiated our second day of not only our new "mask optional" understanding, but also the new expectations for staying in the classroom and being more responsible in choosing times to use the restroom. Yesterday, we did have a small handful of students who decided to "challenge" us and walk out of classrooms without the teacher's permission, but these students were disciplined appropriately. Overall, both yesterday and today, the vast majority of our students seemed accepting of this new expectation, and most appreciated that we have tried to help by adding an extra minute of passing between classes. This challenge will only be defeated, better yet, CONTAINED ... IF the adults in the building continue to enforce the expectation. I am hoping that they can continue to maintain and rally our support without the constant reminder. We will see ...

Another common thread between these first two days after Thanksgiving was the fact that I helped cashier during lunch. I wasn't asked to yesterday, but I made a point to show up near the beginning of the first lunch shift to see how things were going. I noticed someone in "my spot" and in the background our cafeteria manager working one of the lines refreshing the food as the students came through to serve themselves. This never happens; our cafeteria manager is always back in the kitchen and office area "processing" things and putting out fires as they happen throughout each lunch shift. Noting this, I decided that the ladies had to be pretty shorthanded, and I made the decision to take over my cashier stand. My cashier partner revealed to me that they were four short and had to get the help of our Athletic Director (leaving them three short, out of sixteen!). I told the cafeteria manager that they could not be expected to "cover" for three missing staff members. Her response? "I didn't want you to get into any trouble,

Mr. Lasley." I explained to her that getting "into trouble" was the least of my worries and that I would always make myself available (unless I had a meeting scheduled off campus) if they were three or more short and they were already using our Athletic Director. I didn't tell her this, but the very LAST thing we need is to run any more cafeteria staff off because they are being overworked and expected to do more than we would expect ONE individual to do. I will certainly take my chances and help where my help is most needed— at lunch on days like these, it is at the cashier stand ...

One item I had been looking forward to for a while took place on this last day of November– the orientation of a new position that the district had created to help us with our disengaged students and continued issues with absenteeism. Full disclosure: I played a consider-able role in the creation of this position, based on the needs we have identified as we continue to plod through this pandemic quagmire. We needed a full-time person employed to take on some of our most severe cases of student apathy, absenteeism, extreme behavior, and es-pecially the fact that the gap that exists between our white students and minority students has widened over the course of these past two years.

Our guidance counselors' hands are full and have several students with anxiety needs to take care of daily. Our administrators are busy deal-ing with extreme behavior around the building, vandalism and vaping that are taking place at a higher rate than we have ever seen before. The district's temporary placement center for students making poor choices was "booked" with a waiting list. Until we hired the Student Success Coach (SSC), there was NOBODY available to address the fact that too many of our students had not engaged from the begin-ning of the year or have engaged so intermittently that they are still failing some (or ALL) of their classes. As I suspected back in the spring that the trending issues we were seeing were not just going to go away, we must think outside the box and employ whatever resources we have available (or CREATE) to find a way to re-engage our students. Otherwise, we will have failed the students, and ultimately, our community!

As several of us (district as well as Apollo HS personnel) sat around the table in Apollo's conference room debriefing the newly hired SSC on his potential caseload of students, it was a positive and uplifting experience to consider that the "village" had come together for the best interest of a group of students. Would it be easy? Absolutely not! But, these students would have a better chance of success with one person **dedicated** to checking in on them, establishing short-term and long-term goals and break-down barriers to their learning (or meeting their basic needs at home). The best part of this hire was that I have found out that he has already reached out to a good handful of the students on his list and has worked on making a connection. His first official day to start his new role with us? Monday, December 6! ... I feel much better about the chances that these students have already ...

December 3, 2021 – As this busy week after Thanksgiving comes to a close, there are a few things that have become clear and an item or two that has made all the work this week worthwhile. Despite my acceptance that I cannot spend the middle part of my day exclusively at a cash-register helping the cafeteria ladies, I have spent four full and one partial day this week doing just that. I cannot ignore the fact that the ladies need help and have been caught with as many as five personnel short (out of sixteen) this week. It takes a minimum amount of workers to safely get the meals prepared for 1,400 people in our building in a specified amount of time. If we do not get more help provided to our cafeteria staff, I am sure I will be in the same position helping them ... REGARDLESS of how the District Office feels, I am not doing this out of defiance of my supervisor's request; I am doing this based on NEED …

This week, my good friend "Darren" earned a Soaring Eagle Award, which basically gave him a Student-of-the-Month recognition. He was so proud of this accomplishment, he stopped by the office when he found out and he gave me a hug. "Darren" has been holding it together much better since the start of the 2nd 9 weeks. He completes his work, he doesn't stray away, AND he is not heard cackling above all 400 students in the cafeteria during lunch. He is acting more maturely and following instructions given by the adults around him. I am proud of "Darren" and I was happy to tell him so. He DESERVES this recognition …

In our weekly Leadership Meeting, we discussed how this week has gone with the new Restroom Expectations and the fact that we are Mask Optional at the same time. My question posed was, "Can you see a noticeable difference in the hallways during class throughout the day?" While I have only been out of the office and around the building for a short amount of time this week, I have noticed a difference myself, but I need to hear from the folks on the team whose daily work has them traversing all over the building. I was happy to hear that they have noticed a "ghost-town" effect in the halls throughout the day, and teachers are reporting that their classrooms feel more business-like with little interruption. The students seem more "relaxed" and at ease because of their ability to go without a mask. More of our students actually feel inclined to participate! What made this news even more like music to my ears was that our Head Custodian reported NO VANDALISM with the exception of some graffiti on one day. If our new expectation can work for ONE week, there is no reason why we cannot make it work for the rest of this year. THANK YOU, adults and students, for answering my cry for a Rally! Let's keep it up! …

The "topper" to take ALL the feel-good moments I have had was to hear that our teacher who had a near-death experience almost two years ago had a successful surgery today. The stoma in her trachea was successfully removed and she was already talking not long after the surgery!! What a proud and uplifting moment for me and our staff to hear this news! What a BLESSING to have witnessed the transformation we have seen in this teacher as she dedicated herself to achieve this goal. The best part is that we have an opportunity to CONTINUE our work with this "rock star"! I'll take on any number of busy weeks the rest of this year if they all end up as positive as this one …

December 7, 2021 – As I start this day, we continue to hear good news from the hospital where our "rock star" teacher is resting and healing. If she passes the "swallow-test" to ensure everything in her esophagus is functioning correctly and healed enough, she may be released to go home within 48 hours! Again, this is such an uplifting story that keeps all of us grounded at Apollo. We cannot wait to see her return …

On top of a mound of paperwork that seems to creep up at the end of the fall semester, I had made time for a few of us in the Main Office and a couple in the Guidance Office to visit and tour the new building. Only one in the group other than me has been in the new building at all, so this was going to be an eye-opening experience. Considering this, I would have to be patient so that they could "take it all in" and get their questions answered, even though my personal intent is to just check on the progress and see what has changed since my last visit.

Just before we entered the new building, we witnessed furniture being delivered for some of the classrooms. This part of the process is being handled by DCPS Maintenance employees. As we entered the building, the floors in the halls were still filled with dirt, the handrails to all of the steps were still made of 2x4 lumber, and the driveway outside the building was still ungraded dirt. Despite the regular classrooms coming together nicely and pretty much ready to receive furniture with a few small items to button up, the previously mentioned items were TALL tasks that must be completed in order for us to occupy and have students in the building in 28 calendar days! The driveway would take several days alone (with above-freezing temps for the asphalt to set); the handrails would need a lot of welding, finish work, and painting before being usable; the hallways and atrium (foyer to Main Entrance) have a lot of square footage to finish; AND I forgot to mention that the Engineering and Agriculture Academies each need several days of finish work. Needless to say, it is hard for me to visualize ALL these items being 100% complete before January 3rd! But, hopefully, it will be complete enough for us to be able to move in and occupy. In 28 days from today, we will see! ...

Before we toured the new building, I had already been told that the cafeteria ladies desperately needed the assistance of myself and our Athletic Director for lunch. Since Thanksgiving Break, this is the sixth day out of seven that I have helped the ladies for the entire lunch shift due to being short by at least four staff members. Although my supervisor and I had come to an "agreement" that I needed to make myself available to help others (like teachers) during the lunch period, it just does not look as if it will be possible until more help is found for our cafeteria staff. At some point, I am wondering when I will be questioned about this.

The worst part of the lunch experience was that we had two fights break out. One of the fights was between two 9th graders and the other involved upperclassmen. Once again, at least one of the fights was an extreme reaction for something far too simple— one student cut in front of another in the chicken-nugget line.

Although the overall atmosphere that I mentioned has improved since the implementation of our restroom procedures and going mask-optional, we still see too many examples that the mental health of many students has been fractured. It is hard to comprehend that a student feels that they have to start beating on someone just because they cut in front of them in the lunch line(?). What happened to our ability to apply "simple" conflict-resolution strategies as a young adult? Since this past year and having removed our students from schools for the biggest part of the school year, many of our students' coping skills have gone out the window. Twenty-six fights at this point just before the end of the semester is more than we had in the 2019 year altogether …

I am wondering how long it will take to get our students "back" to the same social stature and understanding that they had pre-pandemic? Sadly, it certainly wasn't **_perfect_** back then, but much better than it is right now! As each day unfolds, I come closer to the realization that the **BIGGEST** mistake we made (not that we had much choice at the time) was taking our students out of school …

December 9, 2021 (Sign of the Times) — This week has flashed by at a rapid pace as several end-of-semester events are taking place, we are preparing/boxing for the move into the new building, and I have been putting finishing touches on the Consolidated School Improvement Plan (CSIP). Yesterday, all my work and attention at school got put on HOLD as my wife Angela and I found out that Aaron had another seizure at school. After another lengthy visit to the Emergency Room, we left the hospital at 4:30 pm and our life bounced back to normal for the rest of the evening. We just need to get the combination of meds and Aaron's sleeping patterns in a good place and we hope to not have these high-anxiety, drop-everything emergencies in the future …

Each morning as I am on my way to school, I always get the report for which teachers will be out of the building and whether we have them covered or not. For my 30+ years in education, I have found that Mondays and especially Fridays are ALWAYS the high teacher-absentee days for whatever reason. Most of the absences are truly legit (for illness or child's illness), but some are just putting in for a personal day. At times like these, when stress is at its highest, the Friday absenteeism seems to be more noticeable. Today, we have twelve teachers out of the building (as of the start of the day, at least), which is nearly 15% of our FTE (Full-Time Equivalent) teacher population. This means that our teacher attendance is worse than our student attendance, which we know is NOT good. I am not at all casting judgment on our teachers by saying this; it's the last thing they need at this point. I am just making reference to another challenge that we have to get through days like these; and, YES, this is a "sign of the times" ...

With this in mind, before the school day started, I stopped by the Attendance Office and voiced my pleasure to see our "rock star" Substitute Teachers signing in and getting their plans/duty details. I have mentioned before in this journal how INVALUABLE these retired teachers are for us to be able to pick up and move forward without missing much of a beat on days when we have 15% of our teachers out of the building. Yes, there are a good handful of these individuals that are here nearly EVERY day, and I feel certain there may be adults and especially students who think that they are full-time Apollo employees! Whether they are officially full-time DCPS or Apollo employed, I can tell you that these individuals are 100% Eagle Family members and we do our darndest to remind them of this every opportunity we have! ...

———— ♦ ————

The weather forecast for tonight was for the possibility of tornadic storms across all parts of Kentucky. As the night unfolded, we kept up with the local weather channel and heard the tornado warnings approaching our area. As we are hearing the meteorologist describe what he is seeing on the radar, he explains that the pattern the tornado is making on the screen is due to "heavy debris in the atmosphere". This is a gut-wrenching feeling when you know that the tornado has already leveled houses and communities and it is still making its way in our general direction. As we continue watching the weather late into the evening, we realize that the tornado will end up going well south of us, but we heard enough to know that the community of Mayfield was the town that experienced a direct hit, and there were a handful of small towns that were in the path beyond Mayfield that would have a lot of destruction to wake up to. We will wake up in the morning to find out the total extent of the damage and how close it came to us. We will also need to check on Apollo and the other schools within DCPS to see if any have sustained any damage in the storms.

December 14, 2021 – We could have never imagined the extent of the destruction that we all woke up to on Saturday morning. Seventy-four people confirmed dead in Kentucky alone and the entire town of Mayfield, KY, in Graves County wiped off the face of the earth; match sticks are all that is left. There are 109 residents in Kentucky still unaccounted for …

For many of us Kentuckians who watch the news footage in disbelief, it is hard to consider how our areas were spared when we were so near the path of destruction that also claimed the lives of twelve people in nearby Bremen, KY, in Muhlenberg County. We are so thankful we are picking up small limbs and only having to deal with a power outage for a few hours.

A quick check around Apollo HS showed no damage, and the same was true for all schools within DCPS. All considered, our minds and hearts quickly started to think of what we could do for our neighbors to the south and west, as these school districts had no choice but to close schools for the remainder of this semester while they mourn the losses of loved ones and start clearing out the debris and rubble to make an effort to start rebuilding.

I sent a message out to our leadership team on Sunday to offer my suggestion of taking up a collection at Apollo among staff and any students who would be willing to give, and we send the money directly to the Family Resource Office at Muhlenberg County as an offering of our support. Knowing that there would be other means of assistance (state, federal, local communities) that would be coming their way, we felt that they would have multiple families who would have the need of direct financial support that the money we collect can provide. Since the impact of Covid, the support systems that we normally have in place to quickly provide assistance (like insurance) have slowed down considerably.

Not only did we initiate this collection yesterday AM on ENL, we also honored the victims who were lost to the storms that took place on Friday night with a moment of silence. As I had to be out to attend my uncle's funeral, our lead guidance counselor delivered the message and offered a moment of silence in my absence. As an added boost to my heart broken spirit, there were a handful of clubs around Apollo who had made the decision to take up their own collection of items or money to send to the community of Bremen. It is heartwarming to see that many of these efforts started in the hearts and minds of our **students**. What a powerful and encouraging act for our teens to rise up and consider the needs of others at times of tragedy! One item that keeps weighing heavily on my soul is the fact that this storm did the damage that it did just two weeks before Christmas— a day that families gather, share love, and spend quality time together. Considering this will not be happening for many families who are mourning the loss of loved ones and/or their homes, our collections of money, food, or items is the very least we can do ...

———— ◆ ————

On this Tuesday, I came to school to find that we were in a good place attendance-wise for both students and teachers. The student attendance rate for yesterday was 93.4%, which I am pretty sure was the highest attendance we have recorded since the first week of school in August. We had a total of three teachers out for very legit reasons. I am not sure if the student attendance is due to this being the last week before Finals and Midterm exams this Thursday and Friday (with earning credits OR taking classes over on the line) or anything to do with the work of our new Student Success Coach, but I feel that it is a little of both. Time will tell if this attendance rate continues for today, and tomorrow especially.

As I worked to get caught up on some items that I missed from my absence yesterday, I found that several people needed me for direct conversations that were put on hold. Some of these items involved planning for our next phases of renovations and decisions that need to be made (color of carpet, fabric for chairs in the auditorium, etc.). Due to the fact I know I will not be here beyond the end of this year (nobody else in the building is aware), I make sure to get the input from other people who have a good "eye" for interior decoration. Our CCR Coach and one of our guidance secretaries should honestly have a side job of interior decorating! They would make far more than what they are making in their current roles! Based on *their* input, I recommended a slight variation to what had been initially requested. The architectural designer and construction liaison for DCPS were pleased with "our" choices …

After I got through a series of conversations that were put on hold yesterday, I stopped by the cafeteria to see that the ladies were desperately hoping that I was available to help. They had already made a request for me to be there tomorrow (Wednesday) because this is the day designated for the Apollo Staff Christmas luncheon, and we try to make sure all of our cafeteria ladies rotate during the lunches so that they can enjoy the food the school provides as well. At Apollo HS, we ALL take part in celebrations— our cafeteria workers and custodians are as much a part of the Eagle Family as I am or anyone else! ...

The last bit of news that I heard on this day was from our Lead Ag Teacher, who informed me that they had taken off a lot of scrap metal (most of which were items we were NOT moving to the new building and should have been thrown away years ago!) and was paid over $800 for the load. The BEST part was that they decided to use this money to purchase fencing supplies that would be donated to the Asst. Ag Teacher at Muhlenberg Co. HS, who was one who lived in the Bremen area that lost EVERYTHING and needed to start rebuilding. The fact that our Ag teachers and FFA, again, are the first to think of our neighbors in need makes me feel so proud as the principal of Apollo HS. Our students will learn ___far more___ from this ___gift of giving___ than any gift they may receive in the future. Once again, it is actions like these that are the very least we can do ...

December 17, 2021 (Last Day of the Semester) – This has been a busy week but overall a GOOD week as we have closed out the semester. It has been a shorter week for me due to the funeral I attended on Monday, compressing five days of work into four. Thankfully, because of our altered schedule for midterm and final exams these past two days, my help was not needed (not as many students in the building for lunch) to help cashier so that I was able to get some of my work complete during the lunch period. Yes, my LAST CSIP is "in the books"! ...

Wednesday was a special day for the staff, as we had our annual Christmas Luncheon catered by a local barbeque restaurant. This meal is set up in our library, which is a quiet space where our staff can congregate, eat a GOOD meal (with tons of desserts!), and enjoy each other's company. It's times like these that I can actually overhear our staff talking about things OTHER than work. This is a very positive, uplifting moment for personnel— I just wish we could do things like this more often ...

By Thursday morning, Apollo Staff had collected over $1,200 for the Bremen community. By the end of the day, we had a check processed and written for that amount to be delivered to the Muhlenberg Co. HS Family Resource Center to be distributed as they see fit. I sent a message to all of our staff that I was proud of them for contributing to this very worthy cause and that the Muhlenberg Co. HS Principal and FRYSC were very happy and grateful for the donation.

The only disturbance in the "feel-good moments" on Thursday was that call from Angela to tell me that Aaron had just had another seizure. He was home with her at the time while she was trying to get him ready for school. It didn't last as long as the one he had last Thursday, but it completely wiped him out. Because he came out of it so quickly and he did not hurt himself during the seizure, we decided not to take him in to see his doctor and Angela stayed with Aaron at home. Our obvious concern for Aaron was him having a second seizure in eight days with no understanding of what is causing them. A contact with his neurologist enabled us to move his April appointment to January and an increase in his seizure meds ...

Today started out with a pleasant experience as the Apollo Jazz Band and "AcApollo" Singers played music for our staff and students as they entered the building. This was an AWESOME idea that was presented to me by our Choir Teacher and Band Director. Once again, the easiest part of my job as principal is putting my stamp of approval on these ideas with the simple word "Proceed!". Based on the expressions, the dancing, and the adults/students who stopped by to record or take pictures on their cell phones, I would say this idea and performance was a big hit! One of the last things I did today (before attending our Girl/Boy Doubleheader against one of our town rivals) was to collect my pictures and videos that I had taken this morning in a folder and I shared it to all Apollo Staff with a "Merry Christmas and Happy New Year" message asking for all to enjoy some quality time over the next two weeks. I am betting that some of the staff members will be disappointed they had not seen the live version of the performances! This is something that we can certainly enhance and prepare to do even better for next year ... in Apollo's NEW student and staff entranceway!

Over the past few years I have been principal, even prior to my time at Apollo, I have made an effort to gift those who I have worked closest to at Christmas. In my early years as an administrator, I was not able to do this as much as I wanted, with all of our children still at home. While the gifts I may have purchased were "simpler" back then, I wanted to make an effort to tell those in the office and on my Leadership Team how much I appreciate their hard work and dedication. Sometimes it may have been as simple as a gift card inside a Christmas card with a personal message, but it _**always**_ reflected my thanks for them and what they do for me and the school. This year, I decided that the card I would attach needed to be a THANK YOU card with the usual personal message, followed by a "Merry Christmas". In doing this, I hope that it is even more clear that the gift is NOT intended to be the typical Christmas gift-giving where the expectation is a "return" gift. Does this make a difference? Maybe not. But I want those around me to understand how much their effort and dedication means to me ... and that it has NOTHING to do with Christmas ...

Although my work with students and staff for this first semester has concluded on this Friday, I have some work to put in these next two weeks as I monitor the last details of construction in the new building, the move into the new building, AND the move OUT of the 100's section that will be starting renovation the first week of January. YES, construction will be continuing at Apollo HS as each section of the original building gets renovated and eventually a new cafeteria and kitchen is built. More on these details to come. For now, I will take the peace and quiet that the next two weeks will bring ...

December 21, 2021 (The Move) – Working over Christmas Break is typically a quiet and stress-free atmosphere with very few interruptions from anyone for any work you are completing as principal. Not only that, there were very few times in my past that I would put in a full day at a time. These last two days have been completely different as we are working to ensure that our teachers who are moving into the New Addition are ready for students, AND the same for the teachers who are being temporarily relocated out of the 100's section so that this part of the original building can start being renovated. The only problem is that there is STILL construction to be completed before we can fully take "ownership" and occupancy of our new building ...

Since this past Friday afternoon (including all day Saturday), the DCPS "moving crew" has been busy moving the teachers that have had their items boxed up and their current furniture they need in their new classrooms marked to the new classrooms. Yesterday and today, the moving crew has been moving cart after cart of items and furniture out of the 100's section to the relocated classrooms that have been vacated by teachers moving to the new building. This moving crew has likely each gotten 15,000 steps in each day that they have worked. This move and transition to the new building HAS to happen at this point; ***there is no moving back!*** ...

Upon walking through the new building YESTERDAY, the following items still needed to be complete:

- Handrails installed and finish work on each set of stairs.

- Fixtures completed in some of the restrooms.

- Lights installed in the main entranceway to the building.

- The elevator is not fully functioning and needs some wiring and parts installed before it can pass inspection and be operational.

- Ceiling installed in the entranceway of the building (including drywall, mud, and paint).

- Floor-tile installed in the entranceway and the "Atrium" that connects to the original building.

- Column-wraps around support beams in the Atrium after the floor is complete.

- Lockers installed in the upstairs and downstairs hallways.

- Even worse:

  » Lights, wiring, and ceiling tile is needed in the Engineering Academy (the two main teachers of Engineering have at least two days of non stop moving of items from their current rooms and one full day of set up minimum).

  » Construction "dirt" cleaned up so that we no longer track dirt into the new office spaces and new classrooms. At the point that this is complete, EVERY classroom needs to be set up and cleaned again. THEN teachers can actually set up their classrooms to prepare for instruction and students on Tuesday, Jan. 4th.

  » Our Student Office Entrance to the new building needs to be set up, the offices set up, and proper training for the personnel who will be located in this new section.

  » DCPS Technology needs at least two or three days to have

time to make the final set up of Wi-Fi and technology access for teachers.

» There are other small but time-consuming items that need to be addressed that I have neglected to mention (finishing gutter work, removing construction fence, leveling landscaping areas, etc.).

At our Construction Update Meeting today, we found the dates for "completion" for each item listed above. The floor tile should be complete 12/27 or 12/28. The lockers are to be installed on the same dates. The final cleaning would happen after this and likely 12/29 or 12/30. Lighting and wiring in the Engineering Academy would be complete by 12/28. My problem with this news is that this construction company has completed very few deadlines for tasks that they have mentioned in the past. After today, there are five working days before the new semester begins!

This is my last day to work before Christmas, with my first day to return to Apollo HS for work Monday, Dec. 27. I am very curious to see the work that will be finalized between now and then. I hope I am wrong, but I venture to say that some of the items mentioned in the meeting today will NOT be complete as the contractors mentioned they would. What is normally a relaxing time at work over the holidays has consumed more of my time and especially my thoughts than I have ever experienced in education. What is most frustrating is that this project was originally supposed to be complete and turned over for us by August 1st for us to start this school year in. The 100's area of the original building should be complete as of the end of this semester, and we have just emptied that part of the building to get started! My frustrations are secondary to the frustrations of the DCPS Technology Staff, who will have a day or two to do a week's worth of work. What a mess! ...

December 28, 2021 (The Move Cont'd) – Yesterday was my first day back at Apollo in six days. Although there were only three true working days because of Christmas and the holiday weekend, my hope was to return to see a noticeable difference. Yesterday was the day that I had asked all the teachers who were moving into the new building to start setting up their classrooms. Upon walking into the new building, not only did I NOT notice much that had been completed, but there were classrooms nearest the Atrium that were not accessible because of the hallways getting tiled. Unfortunately, this area would not even be accessible until TOMORROW (Wednesday)... Unbelievable!

We are supposed to have students walking into this new building and new classrooms one week from today! The classrooms are not set up. The wiring for computers is not set up. The hall floors are not complete. The stair steps do not have safety treads in place. Some of the plumbing in the restrooms is incomplete. The ductwork, lighting, and ceiling still need to be completed in the Engineering Academy ... One of our engineering teachers has not moved ANY of his tools, robots, equipment, etc. I just **_cannot_** see us having our semester begin in seven days and the new building fully functioning. Don't forget that we have already committed by relocating teachers from the 100 section of the building to many of the classrooms that teachers of the new building moved out of so that remodeling can take place starting next week! This is a call and a question for someone higher than my rank and pay ...

My first conversation today was a text with the superintendent, asking for us to start considering a "Plan B" for Apollo to start out virtually: the one thing that we were ALL hoping to avoid this year! As much as I hate to admit it or say it, there is NO WAY that we will be able to have students in the new building on January 4th. Even though this reality may be inevitable, the superintendent has asked that we wait until the meeting that will take place at 3:00 pm tomorrow (Wednesday) that will determine whether occupancy can be provided enough for us all to be able to function on the first day of the semester. I have a strong feeling that I will be preparing an unfortunate "virtual instruction until further notice" communication to go out to our staff and our families … and virtual instruction is the LAST thing that our students and staff need right now …

———— ◆ ————

Back in my office after another disappointing visit to the new building, I pulled one of my assistant principals in for a personal and professional conversation. This assistant principal is the one that I have been transitioning to be the "Construction Manager" for Apollo due to the fact that the 100's area we are preparing to remodel starting next week is full of mostly Special Ed. Teachers, and he is the one who supervises them as well as maintains all student IEPs. It only makes sense that as questions come up from the architects or from the contractors that we need input from the teachers who will be working in those spaces, that it is HE that can directly communicate with them and it should not go through me. Little did this assistant principal know that I also had another reason for turning over the Construction Manager role to him …

Inside my office, with the door closed even though nobody else was around, I explained to him my intent to retire at the end of this year. Before I told him, I asked him to keep it between us until further notice and how important that it was to me for it to remain unknown until the right time. I want to be able to continue my job as principal up until the very end of the year and not have to worry about people going to someone else for answers or not paying much attention to my communications, etc. There is a certain degree of this that is going on right now as it is. At the point that everyone knows that the principal is retiring, it is "game on" …

The purpose of this conversation was more than just to help him understand the need to transition someone else into the construction role. Because I will be retiring, there are a lot of decisions that will need to be made about personnel moving into the next year and even policies and procedures where my opinion will be pointless. I need him to keep this in mind as we move into the Spring Semester and the future of Apollo's administration takes a shuffle and personnel in other roles need to be questioned or considered. Again, I will do my part and make decisions that are in the best interest of Apollo HS until my last day, BUT someone else will need to be giving me ***their*** input in making the decisions for Apollo's future.

In this past year (unbeknownst to our Leadership Team), I have been giving more of the hiring of new personnel over to the assistant principals anyway. Because Apollo is a large school with multiple roles to hire each year, we had already shared the responsibility of serving as the "chair" of each hiring committee (with the principal being the person ultimately responsible). This past year, the AP's have served predominantly on every committee to hire personnel for the reason that I have known in the back of my mind that I will be retiring at the end of this year (and those guys probably just thought I was being lazy … LOL!). As I have been drawing to the end of my career (even before the pandemic started), I made the decision to very strategically hand over the reins at the point that it was necessary. I have seen too many administrators carry out what seemed to be their own personal agendas at the end of their careers, and I have told myself that I would not play that game …

As the assistant principal and I finished our conversation, I thanked him for all his work, support, and dedication to our students. I also reminded him that this information about my retirement had to stay between us. I had contemplated telling my children at Christmas, but decided that I should even hold off in telling them until a later date. Not that I do not trust my own children, but there is just too much to risk and someone finding out and sharing with the world on social media. At this point, there are only three individuals who know my intent to retire: this assistant principal, the superintendent, and Angela ...

<u>December 30, 2021 (The Construction MIRACLE ...)</u> – This being my fifth FULL day to work during Christmas Break, I am happy to report that I was WRONG about the new building being complete enough for us to move in with occupancy granted! Miracles CAN happen in the world of construction, AND a tremendous amount of progress can be gained in a 48-hour period. Disaster and Virtual Instruction to start the new semester next week has been AVERTED! ... The building will not be 100% complete, but all parts (classrooms, offices, hallways, restrooms, etc.) that we need to be using will be 100%. There will just be some finishing touches on some of the aesthetic aspects of the Atrium, and they will continue to work on a long list of small items but it will not interfere with any school day. I am SO relieved that I did not have to send the Virtual Instruction communication to staff or families, and I can rest easy over this New Year weekend! ...

On my way out of the building to head home, I was not surprised by a visit by "Tommy" as I approached my truck, the same special young man whom I'd started out helping by squashing the bug that he brought to my attention on the first day of school. NOT surprised by the visit because "Tommy" spends every minute of available daylight (in good weather) riding his bicycle around school and the streets around his house that is located within a block of Apollo's campus. It is not uncommon to be leaving and he will just "happen by" and strike up a quick conversation.

This afternoon, "Tommy" wanted me to know five different things, in rapid-fire fashion, and I was only able to catch one of the items he mentioned. He pointed out that he had shaved his "mustache" and he didn't seem very happy about it (chances are that he had been forced by his guardians to shave for the holidays). I took the opportunity to cheer "Tommy" up by telling him not to worry and that he can always grow it back.

As "Tommy" acknowledged this and started to pull away, I stopped him because I noticed the tread on his bicycle tires was completely bald. As I mentioned, "Tommy" rides his cruiser bicycle ALL the time. Although he doesn't ever go beyond "cruise" speed, the number of miles he has put on those tires has obviously taken a toll. I pointed this out to "Tommy" and mentioned to him that we are going to get his bicycle tires replaced (he had already quickly mentioned that he could not afford new tires). To this he said, "Thank you," and pulled away, telling me to "have a good evening" ...

Just before leaving, I texted the following to my two assistant principals:

On another note... 1. **Tommy** stopped as I was leaving to inform me that he had shaved his mustache - I told him not to worry, he can always grow it back... 2. We need to get **Tommy** new tires for his bike....

AFTERWORD

Humanity in Peril ...

This "can" has been kicked long enough ... If you have read this far, I am hoping you will read a little more. The following serves as a summary of issues that have been presented in this journal that need immediate attention by society (parents, members of the community, legislators):

* The pipeline delivering quality educators to the schools across our nation needs to be made **_full_** again! This is a very complicated fix, but it is at a critical status, pandemic or not. The pandemic has only made this worse.

  » We **_must_** start treating educators as professionals and with the respect that they have **_always_** deserved. I have had the pleasure of working with many very hard working professionals who have dedicated their lives to their careers— all for the cause of children's future success. The connections I have emphasized within this journal pale in comparison to the positive examples I have seen in my career and continue to see to this day. There are obviously bad examples of teachers who have mistakenly chosen education for their career (just as there are for any career choice). Of those whom I have worked with over 32 years, I can safely say that the inadequate teachers represent less than 5% of the population. Most of the teachers I have had the pleasure to work with would agree in saying "We **_love_** our kids and we will always try to make decisions for what we feel is *__in their best interest__.*" We need parents to start giving teachers the benefit of the doubt and at the very least have a conversation with them first before complaining to the principal (or straight to the top with the superintendent). The education of our nation's children was meant to be a *__partnership__*, and with healthy partnerships there always exists a certain amount of TRUST. I have had too many negative conversations in this past year with parents, and this journal exposes several events where there clearly is no trust or respect demonstrated.

» Too many teachers and especially classified individuals (custodians, cafeteria staff, bus drivers, etc.) work *__second__* jobs just to make ends meet. The cost-of-living increases that have been experienced in most other sectors of society have not been afforded educators (at least in Kentucky) for over ten years now. With inflation on the rise again, this only makes it harder. Our nation's legislators MUST realize this! If education is truly the "Gateway to Humanity", then *__education should be a TOP priority__* and should not depend upon political affiliation. Most educators have attained at least a master's degree by the time they are twenty years in, and some have earned thirty credit hours and a specialist certification beyond that. It is time that educators get paid what they deserve.

» With new concerns in education, such as the mental health and social-emotional wellness of our students, racial tensions, etc., our teachers need training. With training comes the need for resources and budgets for districts to support the needs that exist.

• Broken Students/Broken "Partnerships" – I have already mentioned the notion of the partnership that is *__supposed__* to exist between the school (more directly, the **_teachers_**) and the parents or guardians of our students. The pandemic has created even more "lost souls" walking our halls or chronically absent from school than ever before. This partnership has always been tougher at the high school level than the lower grades, and this journal has emphasized moments when Apollo's attendance rate (not counting students who are quarantined!) has been high-80's. We cannot have ANY influence (academically or emotionally) on a student who is not in front of us. By and large (as it has always been), there is a direct correlation between our students who are failing or struggling the most and their attendance.

Taking this one step further, we also have more "lost souls" than ever before whose attendance IS good but they are walking the halls and sitting in our classrooms with no purpose to do anything more than to exist. Our mid-year failure reports showed the number of students failing multiple classes and even ALL classes near **_double_** than what we have experienced in "normal" times. Our district alternative school cannot take all these kids, so our leadership team at Apollo is left trying to think even further outside the box to find a way to make these students successful (that happens to be the **_very_** challenge that I have given the dynamic leadership team here at Apollo— "epiphanies" are ALWAYS welcome on my team!). The biggest part of this problem is the lack of a positive adult presence at home and the completely broken aforementioned partnership. That is one of the biggest changes that I have seen over the course of the past fifteen years or more. There are far more students in our schools NOT being raised by either one of their parents. Regardless of this fact, society's households MUST find a way to strengthen the partnership with schools again. This is a **_societal_** issue and the **_future of humanity depends on this being corrected_**!

- There is too much hatred and general negativity in the world! I have little use (those who know me would use the word "miniscule" or "doesn't exist") for social media due to the fact that these platforms are the breeding grounds for the hatred, the negativity, and the misleading information that most of society hangs its hat on. You can try to find me within these social media platforms, but there will be only one that I even have an account on ... and the sole reason I have the account is for informational purposes ONLY and the hopes that I can land some free gear from my favorite university (actually true!). For any good that *may* exist within social media platforms, the negative FAR outweighs the positive. Think of what it takes to get blocked from using social media and the horrible examples our nation has been exposed to... our children **see** this! Since the existence of social media, we have seen more broken children who have experienced trauma as a direct result of being bullied on social media. The sad thing is that our children are only mirroring what they have seen among adults (parents, public officials, and even the famous people they idolize). How can we expect anything different from our children? If education is the "Gateway to Humanity," then I firmly believe that social media will be the "***downfall of society***", and I, for one, absolutely ***refuse*** to take part in it. Again, this is a ***societal*** issue and the ***future of humanity depends on this being corrected***!

- Violence and extreme behavior in our youth— the examples depicted in my journal entries are ***typical*** among schools in our nation, and there are many schools that experience ***far worse***. Combining all of these bulleted categories, can anyone out there say that educators are overpaid for what they do? I am fully aware there are some who actually would! The pandemic has changed ALL of us and our students are the perfect example of the effects of isolation, the continued barrage of negativity, the removal of true learning as well as the ability to participate in extracurricular activities. And yes, even some of our parents have been highlighted in this journal to have a very quick "charge the capital" reaction that could easily be resolved by a simple and respectful conversation. Our children need some dedicated time to HEAL emotionally from what they have experienced these past two years. Educators need to be given the training **_and_** the resources (physical as well as _human_), and districts MUST dedicate time within school days to work on healing our children. As I mentioned to Apollo's Leadership Team one Friday morning, if the pandemic ENDED tomorrow, it would take educators several years to overcome the collective damage that has been done for teaching and learning to resemble in any way what it looked like in the Fall of 2019.

- The damage demonstrated throughout this journal has taken its toll on too many "rock star" teachers. Regardless of any promise of increase in pay, my fear, based on what I am seeing at Apollo HS and what I am hearing within our region (as well as what I am reading across the nation!), tells me that there will be a record number of teachers either retiring, retiring early, or just leaving the profession at the end of the 2022 school year. **_The future of humanity depends on me being WRONG and this being corrected moving forward! ..._**

Before I conclude and before anyone turns my comments into something political, I am AMERICAN and refuse to fully associate with any one party (there is far too much partisanship in our country these days). The days of respecting others for their opinion and the ability to still shake hands may have gone completely. The same can be said for making decisions for what is in the best interest of the citizens of our country. Instead, there are too many decisions being made to just oppose the other party. Those are not at all the beliefs that our country was founded upon. Like education, the health and safety of the citizens of our country should **_never_** be a partisan issue ...

———◆———

In closing, I would venture to say that nearly everyone reading this journal had an adult (in some cases, **_several_**) who made a positive impact on them when they were in school, and that "connection" was instrumental in helping them become WHO they are today. Let's go further and just consider the collective K– 12 academic preparation that any reader would say made a direct influence on the career or profession that they chose. How many readers would say that they wish they **_had given more attention_** to their K– 12 educational experience and how much that would have impacted what they are doing now? **_Let's all agree that the future of our nation and the future of society, in general, lies within the capable hands and hearts of EDUCATORS_**!! If this statement is true, wouldn't education be a **_worthy investment_** ??? …

Legislators, parents, community members, listen up!! Education NEEDS your help and deserves your RESPECT/SUPPORT! The "alarm" has been sounding for many years now. In the writing and publishing of this journal, I have merely increased the volume. Please help answer the call ! …

CPSIA information can be obtained
at www.ICGtesting.com
Printed in the USA
LVHW100234150722
723595LV00010B/41